USING BLOGS TO ENHANCE LITERACY

The Next Powerful Step in 21st-Century Learning

Diane Penrod

Rowman & Littlefield Education
Lanham, Maryland • Toronto • Plymouth, UK
2007

Published in the United States of America
by Rowman & Littlefield Education
A Division of Rowman & Littlefield Publishers, Inc.
A wholly owned subsidiary of The Rowman & Littlefield Publishing Group, Inc.
4501 Forbes Boulevard, Suite 200, Lanham, Maryland 20706
www.rowmaneducation.com

Estover Road
Plymouth PL6 7PY
United Kingdom

British Library Cataloguing in Publication Information Available

Library of Congress Cataloging-in-Publication Data

Penrod, Diane.
    Using blogs to enhance literacy : the next powerful step in 21st-century
learning / Diane Penrod.
        p.   cm.
    Includes bibliographical references and index.
    ISBN-13: 978-1-57886-565-9 (hardcover : alk. paper)
    ISBN-13: 978-1-57886-566-6 (pbk. : alk. paper)
    ISBN-10: 1-57886-565-4 (hardcover : alk. paper)
    ISBN-10: 1-57886-566-2 (pbk. : alk. paper)
    1. English language—Discourse analysis.   2. English language—
Rhetoric—Study and teaching—Data processing.   3. Computers and
literacy.   4. Discourse analysis, Literary.   5. Communication—
Technological innovations.   6. Literary form.   I. Title.
    PE1422.P46   2007
    808'.0420285—dc22   006031324

For my former undergraduate students Tina, Patricia, Rebecca, and Sean; my former graduate students Jenn R., Gary, Karen, Leigh, Linda, Melissa, and Stefanie; and teachers everywhere who "get tech," like Bill, Age, Roberta R., Joanna, Lara, and Olga.

Each is making a difference in helping people become literate in the 21st century.

CONTENTS

Preface   vii

1   Why Blog?   1

2   Blogging and New Literacies   19

3   Blogs as a New Writing Genre   35

4   Gender and Blogging   49

5   Ethnicity and Blogging   63

6   Blogs and Bullying   77

7   Encouraging Safe Blogging Practices   95

8   Integrating Multiple Intelligences and Blogging   119

9   Creating Classroom Ethics for Blogging   139

10 Blogging Matters   151

References   167

Subject Index   171

Name Index   173

About the Author   175

PREFACE

When I was younger, the world was grounded in an industrial-based economy. My family and friends saw themselves working in the Rust Belt's steel mills, auto factories, and refineries after their senior year of high school. College wasn't a necessity for someone to have a prosperous life. In those days, a person could go from graduation to grave working for the same employer with a living wage, good benefits, and job security.

Then something happened just months after my college graduation in 1980: The American economy bottomed out. I stood in an unemployment line with attorneys, factory workers, and business executives. The grand employers in upstate New York—Bethlehem Steel, General Electric, Buffalo Forge, Cargill, and the like—folded under the weight of a stagnant economic structure. America moved toward a service economy, and the great jobs and years of company loyalty many of us expected upon entering the workforce became a thing of the past.

Some of us from those early days of America's economic transformation were able to adapt to the ebb and flow; others, regardless of race or initial social position, suffered greatly. As comedian Stephen Colbert observed during his 2006 commencement speech at Knox College in Illinois,

> The world is waiting for you people with a club. Unprecedented changes happening in the last four years. Like globalization. We now live in a hyperconnected, global, economic, outsourced society. Now, there are positives and minuses here. . . . [W]hen you enter the workforce, you will find

competition from those crossing our all-too-poorest borders. Now I know
you're all going to say, "Stephen, Stephen, immigrants built America."
Yes, but here's the thing—it's built now. I think it was finished in the mid-
'70s sometime. At this point it's a touch-up and repair job (June 3, 2006).

Colbert is on target. America *is* built now, it *was* finished in the mid-
1970s, and the "touch-up and repair job" that seems to happen on a
fairly regular basis nowadays often comes at the expense of those not
prepared to meet the challenge. My generation, the ones who gradua-
ted from high school and college beginning in the mid-1970s, felt Colbert's club first. Today, the club swings harder, faster, and sooner. All
too frequently, students and new graduates are the ones who find themselves face-to-face with the unpredictable economic club Colbert described.

Thirty years after the creation of the Rust Belt, America's economy
finds itself once again in flux. The promise of a robust service economy
has been outsourced elsewhere. But the information age has taken hold,
creating the "information highway" and once again transforming
America—this time into a globalized knowledge economy.

While not too long ago it was possible for an American to hold a ter-
rific job with a high school education, nowadays learning cannot stop
with twelve years of basic schooling. College, either at the two- or four-
year level, seems virtually mandatory for anyone to obtain meaningful
work. In industry, the drive exists to ensure that youngsters become
smart, agile, and flexible future workers. And as most current employees
can attest, lifelong learning dominates discussions, as employers seek
ways to develop and maintain a skilled human capital base in light of
global competition.

Technology is at the core of today's knowledge economy. Savvy participants in a knowledge economy understand how technology works to
streamline various tasks. But our full understanding of technology extends beyond the surface knowledge of how to harness available technology to make a job easier or more efficient. When someone has
complete command of technology, he or she recognizes the quality and
the relevance of certain technologies over others in different circumstances.

For me, blogs (short for web logs) represent a command of technology literacy in that broader sense. In a global, information-driven, technologically infused society, blogging is an illustration of how to control available technologies in relevant ways. Many users have come to recognize quality blogs versus superficial ones and the evolution of blogging as technology changes.

If I were to ask a teenager about quality vs. superficial blogs, the two of us could wax all day on what makes a blog worthy. Perhaps to some, the discussion would be mundane if not banal. But our discussion would be neither dull nor trite. Talking about blogs with teenagers demonstrates how economic, sociocultural, and historical realities shape learning in this new information system. Those who cannot perform in the blogosphere will be left behind, just as many of my friends, family members, and acquaintances were when America's economy shifted from industry to service (and then again when the service economy changed to a knowledge-driven one).

This is a crucial point. Information and communication technologies (ICT) are the cornerstones of the knowledge economy. Because contemporary adolescents grow up surrounded by ICT and become reliant on the technologies that connect to their lives, a book that focuses on preteens and teenagers using blogs as a way to enhance literacy makes sense. In 2005, the World Bank reported that while ICT access shows promise for expansion and enhancing learning while maintaining quality and relevance in students' lives, problems still exist (Hepp, Hinostroza, Laval, & Rehbein, 2005). Those concerns are linked to educator training and parental information rather than electronic capability.

If educators and parents are not paying attention to the greater significance blogs have for student growth in a knowledge economy, perhaps Stephen Colbert has an extra club so we can join in the next beatdown. Certainly someone has to point out to adults that blogs are a crucial component of 21st-century literacy. Students clearly understand what is at stake: Blogs are not the answer to developing students' information literacy; they are the herald, the harbinger, of what is to come regarding literacy in a global knowledge economy.

This book was born from my own experience in teaching students—primarily preservice writing teachers but also typical undergraduates, graduate students, and veteran teachers—how to integrate technology, particularly blogging, into the writing process. In 2003 I began to teach students about blogging. My focus was more than lecturing on the "how tos" connected with setting up a blog. Such an approach would take little more than thirty minutes and leave me with little else to do for a 140-minute class period over fifteen weeks. Instead, my approach was grounded in how blogs have become the foundation—what I call later in this book a "killer app"—for changing the ways in which professionals and novices write and think.

Whether my students examined how journalism has evolved in the blogosphere or how students learn in asynchronous environments like blogs, the result always returned to the same place: What was once information has transformed into knowledge. In the 1990s it was enough for a user to gather data; in the 21st century, the user has to know how to manipulate facts, statistics, or other types of content to make meaningful materials that wide-ranging audiences can access. This book, then, addresses many of the issues my classes have taken up in our discussions and explorations into the blogosphere and how it has shaped our understanding of literacy.

Because literacy is a complex topic, as are the social aspects of blogging, to intersect the two creates a host of issues. To that end, I have based chapters on contemporary concerns. My hope is to make the material relevant to educators and parents who want to learn more about the blogging phenomenon beyond what is described in the mainstream media. Rather than tackle these topics in a sensationalized manner, so often the format used in daytime TV, morning newspaper headlines, and national news weeklies, I strive to provide in-depth research as to the reasons why particular subjects like cyberbullying, gender differences, and race occur in the blogosphere. As I tell my classes, the Internet is an extension of everyday life; it has been created by humans, so cyberspace contains both the best and the worst of who we are.

My indebtedness to my undergraduate and graduate students in finishing this project extends far beyond anything I can describe here. They deserve the credit for this book. They have cajoled me to begin this work, contributed many ideas that readers will find throughout the pages, pushed me to complete the project when deadlines loomed and their papers needed grading, and cheered me when my research slowed. My students' interest in this topic sometimes exceeded my own—a point that more than a few will find hard to believe, I am sure. Still, it is true.

In the process of writing this book, I have come to realize why so many of them wanted me to finish: It represents their world, the lives they live, the schooling they want others to have. Whether my students were teachers, preservice teachers, or potential writers, so many of them believed in this project and contributed graciously of their time, their ideas, and their support. While any mistakes in the book are mine alone, I see the finished product as a shared effort between me and dozens of collaborators, some real and others virtual.

1

WHY BLOG?

Blog (short for we*b log*) is the latest buzzword in the media, cyberspace, and teenagers' discourse. *Blog* here. *Blog* there. Journalist *blogs*. Political *blogs*. Confessional *blogs*. Soldier *blogs*. It seems the word *blog* now appears everywhere in popular culture. Some first-graders even know the word *blog*, although most have yet to start blogging. Indeed, blogs are the world's hottest, fastest-growing electronic medium for writing and distributing opinions and information. National weekly magazines, trade papers, academic journals, local television news programs, and radio talk shows have all weighed in on the blogging phenomenon. Businesses, newspapers, and probably even Granddad have blogs.

Many people between the ages of ten and twenty have at least one blog. That means the youngsters and young adults who surround you are blogging. Regularly. Religiously. Most of the time, these young bloggers are writing before, after, and sometimes during school hours; in the wee hours; and without adult supervision. For preteens, teens, and young adults, blogging has generated a subculture that few adults enter.

In schools and colleges, blogs have been linked to an increase in both Internet use and adolescent misbehavior. Yes, blogs create hot type. A news outlet looking for a quick, sensational story about blogging does not have to search far for attention-grabbing ideas. Dozens of spectacular stories abound, each one seemingly more lurid, sinister, and foreboding than the last when it comes to youngsters and blogs.

If they are following only news reports, however, educators and parents are missing an important point about blogging: Blogs and blogging motivate students to read and write. While many negative stories about blogs are genuine, there are an equal number of success stories, show-ing how students' literacy thrives in a multimedia culture.

So with all this press coverage, why are many teachers, professors, and parents feeling incredibly out of the information loop when it comes to blogging? And, perhaps more importantly from an educational standpoint, why do educators and parents know so little about why stu-dents want to blog? Actually, the answers to both questions are con-nected. Part of the answer relates to *cultural lag*, a phenomenon best described as aspects of culture that advance at different rates with vary-ing social groups. In particular, cultural lag connects to major advance-ments in technology; it takes nearly two or three decades for most people in society to catch up to the early adopters and the children, whose lives are immersed in new technology. Because blogging is only a few years old and primarily a form of youth subculture communication, blogging is often a blip on most adults' computer screens.

But blogs and blogging need to be more than a keyword search in Google, and here's why. Depending on your age, gender, ethnicity, eco-nomic standing, and geographic location as well as your overall interest in technological change and growth, cultural lag can be relatively short or long in duration. Meanwhile, the rate and speed with which technol-ogy evolves continues. This is why blogs and blogging are current topics and why they might transform into another equally hot topic about writ-ing, literacy, and learning in the near future. Teachers and parents can stave off some effects of cultural lag by reading and learning more about technological advances in literacy, like blogs, so they can become more familiar with the activities in which their students or children engage while online.

This chapter—as well as this book—is dedicated to helping those readers who feel undereducated and overwhelmed by the concept of blogging understand the rush to blog that is occurring in local schools, colleges, and universities and students' rooms all across America and the world. In the pages that follow, my goal is to give teachers, professors, and parents some insight into why students are blogging, how blogging can advance literacy skills by becoming a new writing genre, whether there are gender differences in how we blog, how to keep students safe in the blogosphere, and what happens when teachers, professors, and students have personal blogs to express their thoughts and those sites conflict with their home institutions. The book concludes by creating ethics—an ethos, if you will—for classroom-based blogging.

FIVE BASIC REASONS

For now, though, let's discuss five reasons why this blog storm has happened in society. While there are a variety of reasons why an individual blogger chooses this medium, the specific impulse generally falls into one of five areas:

1. Blogs are incredibly easy to publish because of technological advances.
2. Blogs mix pleasure with information to create an information reformation.
3. Blogs are a malleable writing genre.
4. Blogs allow writers to generate new personas and construct new worlds.
5. Blogs empower those who are often marginalized in society.

If you blog or if you know someone who blogs regularly or has his or her own blog, think of the reasons you, a friend, or a child engage in the blogging experience. While the answers are probably a mix of the five aspects presented here, more likely one or two motivations form the basis. So let's explore these motives a little further.

They Are Incredibly Easy to Publish

Many people write, but few writers ever move toward publishing a book. Some estimates put the figure at 1 or 2 percent for writers who publish a manuscript, even though those who write number in the thousands if not hundreds of thousands. For these hopeful authors, the journey of seeing one's words in print is often dashed by the expense and effort it takes to produce a worthwhile book.

Even if an author considers a print-on-demand service or vanity press as a venue for his or her work, a harsh realization soon sets in: Turning a manuscript into a sellable book is often a time-consuming and expensive process. Moreover, writers discover that there are many intervening voices, from editors and agents to marketing staffs, publicity directors, and reviewers, who shape the final product. As a result, the author's voice becomes blended with the voices of many others, some of whom have more control over the finished piece than the original author.

Because book publishing is time- and cost-consuming and because a book's success depends on multiple cultural, social, and economic factors, and because not all ideas merit publication, editors and agents screen submitted ideas for their viability as finished books. In short, editors and agents are gatekeepers. They work with writers to shape books that people will purchase based on the cultural, social, and economic factors that determine sales. This is sometimes a harsh lesson for writers to learn.

Like many hopeful authors, students also face similar struggles in having their writing—their voices—recognized. All too often these days, students' writing is school-based, composed in response to a state assessment prompt, a college entrance essay request, or some other academic demand. In these situations, the joy of writing is not emphasized; writing is generated with an explicit purpose. The minutiae of grammar, word choice, and topic appropriateness are juxtaposed against whatever creativity a student writer can muster in a twenty-five-minute writing session. As with expectant authors, students' successes in school-based writing are also influenced by multiple cultural, social, and economic factors.

Ultimately, like a promising manuscript, student writing will be noticed and judged based on its worthiness. Student efforts are labeled as "good" or "bad" writing, "proficient" or "deficient." Whatever judgments are rendered by teachers, exam scorers, or admissions personnel will determine students' success or placement in their educations. Like their authorial counterparts, student writers face excruciatingly high-stakes decisions made about the words they write on a piece of paper. In the writing field, gatekeepers can be harsh taskmasters.

Both hopeful authors and student writers aim to please the sets of nameless, faceless readers who critique the writing in front of them. Success brings a flood of approval, esteem, and respect; failure brings forth an equally compelling set of negative emotions. All writers must do (in either experience) is garner the gatekeeper's endorsement of the finished product. Suddenly, it might seem clearer why blogging is in demand.

Blogging needs none of these gatekeeping practices. A writer who is semi-proficient with computer technology can set up a blog in about fifteen to thirty minutes and mass distribute his or her ideas the same day. With blogging technology tools and software like Blogger, Xanga, MySpace, Moveable Type, and WebCrimson, a writer can go from keyboard to public in a matter of seconds. Since there is no outside editor or agent to act as an idea clearinghouse and no teacher or examiner to disapprove of language and topic choices, a writer can type, click, and publish. The process really is that simple. A person can begin blogging and publishing within minutes. An opinion can be formed, keyed into the software, and uploaded for public viewing in the time it takes to brew a pot of coffee.

However, just because someone has the technical ability to blog within minutes does not make that person a savvy blogger. Nor does such technological ease in spreading one's thoughts make the thoughts more respected, praiseworthy, or valuable. All the technology does is makes the publication process simpler and more direct. If a writer's talent or ability is weak, or if the writer's ideas are flawed in some way, technology only provides a faster, more public venue for exposing those mistakes or vulnerabilities.

When I speak with students and teachers about blogging, I like to compare the blogging process to backgammon. Both are easy to learn but hard to master. And successful blogging is similar to success at backgammon in that both take some skill and luck, but even more they take imagination, intuition, an aesthetic sense, and a bit of insight. For novices, blogging and backgammon take little equipment to start, a general but often murky objective, and some rudimentary understanding of why one starts where he or she does. As newbies become more involved with either process, they realize that to become proficient they must understand the prevailing rules and principles. It is then that bloggers and the backgammon players discover that excellence in either endeavor depends on creativity and engagement. Neither is an activity for the passive spectator.

To blog well, as to play backgammon well, you must make the time as well as develop the desire and interest needed for expertise. The simplicity in a game of backgammon belies the strategies and tactics one must develop to become a skilled player. Similarly, the effortlessness and straightforwardness of blogging technology does not ensure a successful blogging experience. Without a solid foundation in the skills, strategies, tactics, and aesthetics of composing the written word, writers rarely become master bloggers. Or, to put this in simpler terms, just because someone can blog doesn't mean he or she should.

The backgammon analogy explains why so many people start blogs but never continue them. They are easy to start but challenging to master, and maintaining a blog is a commitment a writer makes with an audience. In a 2004 Pew Internet study, Lee Rainie estimated that 3.8 million people have started blogs but nearly 60 percent of them are abandoned within a year. Within the past year alone, more than 900,000 blogs emerged in cyberspace. The allure of publishing one's thoughts diminishes over time unless writers feel the passion or commitment to blogging on a regular basis.

Although the ease of user technology makes blogging appealing for beginners, the trick is to learn how to master the skills and the forms necessary for success. Just as with playing backgammon, blogging is a process of fits and starts, of breaking unknown rules and learning from one's mistakes, of refining and honing one's skill through trial, error, and continual practice. Over time, novice bloggers who catch on become confident bloggers. The effortlessness with which confident bloggers write happens over time and with much practice. The technology is simply the vehicle that allows the words and ideas to become public.

They Mix Pleasure with Information

The second reason why some individuals blog leads us to blogging's "pleasure principle": *Blogito ergo fun*. I blog because it's fun. Blogging is a way cool activity. For a writer, there is no bigger kick than giving one's words and ideas life and sending them out to be read. The pleasure of immediate publication, which is what happens with a blog, appeals to a good number of writers. As I mentioned earlier, from thought to keyboard to dissemination, a blog posting can be up and out into the public in as few as five minutes. That's certainly much faster than seeing one's words in a letter to the editor, a commentary piece, an article or a book, where time from acceptance to publication can take anywhere from a few days to a year or more. In our hurry-up world, some writers want to see their words in print, in public, as soon as possible. A week, a month, or a year later just won't do.

For impatient teens, the instant publication factor is a major draw. So too is the idea that blogging is playing with language, finding pleasure in writing. This aspect of the writing process is often missing in school-based writing, with its emphasis on skill acquisition, mechanics, and state standards. The lack of play in classroom writing activities draws students to blogging for several important reasons—all connected to learning.

Educational psychologists explain that when we integrate play or pleasure with a learning activity, we tend to become more engaged in the material and retain a greater amount of information. A sense of play allows us to tap into our creativity. Because blogging doesn't necessarily feel like writing, especially not like school-based writing, students find themselves often experiencing what psychologist Mihalyi Cszikszentmihalyi (1990) calls "optimal experience" or "flow."

In flow, bloggers enter into a Zen-like state, a "zone" in common usage, where they are caught up in the moment and time slips away. Many students have told me that when they are really engaged in blogging, hours slip by as if they were minutes or seconds. These student bloggers describe the interactivity of blogging—mixing multiple modalities of visual images, written text, sounds, colors, and so forth—as being the primary reason why they feel time escapes them. Well-constructed blogs offer multiple levels of physical and mental stimulation for users. Consequently, bloggers find themselves continually drawn into deeper layers of the blogosphere, searching for new information to include on their sites.

But what draws bloggers deeper into the blogosphere, and how do creativity and learning connect with this process? When a blog functions at its peak, several elements are at work to encourage writers to play, to be creative, and to continue blogging:

There is a clear reason. Writers usually have a set reason for blogging. It might be that they want to engage in punditry, self-expression, confessional writing, or some other form of prose or poetry writing. Regardless, they have a purpose for constructing and maintaining a blog that guides each step of the creative process.

There is immediate feedback. Bloggers thrive on response, so comments that are left indicate how well they have done with particular entries. Most orphaned blogs are ones that have had no response whatsoever.

There is a balance between challenge and skill. Bloggers need to feel that a balance exists between the challenge of and skill in generating and maintaining a blog. If a blogger believes the challenge to maintain a blog is too great or if he or she lacks the skill to do so, then boredom, anxiety, or abandonment set in and the writer moves on to other practices where the balance between challenge and skill is better.

There is focused concentration. As long as there is continual feedback, a sense of balance between challenge and skill, and clarity of purpose for blogging, a writer will center on the task at hand. Otherwise, a blogger's concentration becomes preoccupied with other ideas and the interest in blogging is diffused into other activities.

There are limited distractions. When bloggers are able to center themselves in the here-and-now, it allows their minds to focus on the blog, and optimal experiences occur. If distractions take over the moment, such as pressing family worries, health issues, or school problems, then they lose interest unless they find ways to discuss these issues on their blogs.

There is no fear of failure. Bloggers find the blogging process fun because there is little reason to fear failure: Their challenges and skills are compatible with the experience, they are clear in what needs to be done at each stage of the process, and they feel comfortable and in control of the moment. In addition, there is no gatekeeper grading the blog as "pass" or "fail." Because there is no fear of failure, bloggers find themselves taking risks in their writing that they would never try in a print-based or school environment. As a result, many student bloggers describe their writing experiences as liberating and growth-enhancing.

There is little to no self-consciousness. Bloggers feel as though they are part of a larger entity or community, which permits them to drop many of the self-censoring behaviors people develop in real life. When bloggers are in the "zone" of blogging, self-consciousness disappears and the writing takes on a life of its own. Bloggers often develop a different online personality or persona that reflects this identity change.

There is time distortion. When bloggers write, hours seem like minutes and minutes seem like nanoseconds. When bloggers hit their creative peak, or *flow*, their sense of real time becomes altered and they believe time has passed more or less quickly than it actually has.

There is an increase in autotelic behavior. When bloggers enjoy the act of blogging, the activity becomes an end to itself. Bloggers start to blog just for the sake of blogging. In other words, if they find themselves in the zone, they write without having a particular goal in mind other than finding enjoyment in the moment. They take the time and care to select certain words or phrases to describe emotions, events, and experiences that are often glossed over in print exercises. These writers spend time crafting their ideas before uploading because they feel a sense of responsibility to their readership.

So committed bloggers build and maintain blogs because it is a purely pleasurable experience for them. Creativity emerges from a blog's novelty, and the medium is different from other writing genres. But a blog's uniqueness wears thin quickly without a purpose for composing entries. Consequently, once bloggers decide on a reason for blogging, the creative process is engaged. They have problems to solve, a desire to disseminate new information or knowledge, a desire to compose, and a potential audience to entertain. Bloggers have a passion to pursue. Blogs become a place to play out aspects of their passion.

Every playground needs playmates to provide feedback, and a blog is no exception. Without responding voices, bloggers have no idea how well they are doing. In a sense, without commentary, bloggers have unrequited passion. As we know from most stories, when passion goes unanswered, frustration sets in and disappointment and discouragement occur. When a blogger gives up in frustration, discouraged from the lack of posts, the blog becomes orphaned. The most likely cause for blog abandonment is a lack of response—recognition from others of the work the blogger has put into the site.

An informal study I conducted with several undergraduate classes over the past four years suggests that the number-one reason why students orphan their blogs is because no one ever posted a comment. There was no trace of anyone coming to see the blogger's efforts. The blogger's passion goes unreturned. Over time, a lack of feedback sends a message to bloggers that their work is simply a waste of time. In turn, these disgruntled bloggers become disenchanted with blogging and they miss out on the optimal experience other bloggers seem to have. Their blogs become a disappointment, a source of pain. Good-bye, cruel blog.

But what exactly misfires on some blogs and not others? The playfulness and pleasure experienced by successful bloggers leads us to a type of information reformation—a different organization of information. Instead of the linear structures you find in books, a blog's information is "chunked" and linked in rhizomatic or root-like shapes that branch into numerous directions and lead to infinite patterns of ideas and knowledge. Visitors can move about on a blog in any number of directions and learn something new. If visitors find information presented in a linear, print-based manner, they tend to shy away from investigating the content. In short, savvy bloggers take their passion and transform it so others can share it.

If you were to create an outline of a blogger's postings, with its representative links and comments, you would most likely see multidirectional paths leading to bits and pieces of knowledge. These patterns would look something like a tree's root system. Instead of moving in a progressive, linear path, bloggers can move in any number of directions, taking readers with them and then allowing the readers to go off on their own paths.

These rhizome-like mental models arrange information differently. Instead of the traditional sequential, spatial, or convergent mental models that dominate much of pedagogical or educational discourse, these rhizomatic mental models are grounded in serendipity, in the bloggers' or readers' pleasurable interests. The patterns of learning have an internal, perhaps idiosyncratic, purpose that connects to an individual's own interests rather than being a system of reward and punishment. This is where autotelism—an event or entity valued for its own sake—becomes clearest in the blogging process.

Changing mental models for processing information is but one characteristic of the information reformation happening in the blogosphere. Another element of this reformation is a common language. In the blogosphere, writers often borrow heavily from the text message or instant message (IM) phenomenon. IM speak, or texting language, is not scholarly. Rather, the vocabulary, grammar, and syntax come from the users' needs and not from an official source. Whenever an official source is needed, a bloggers need only provide a link to somewhere on the Internet to offer up proof for their statements.

Such linguistic and procedural changes are driven by the ease of and speed with which blogging technology moves. Bloggers have been pushed to create a common language that differs from academic prose because of faster computer processing times, smaller writing spaces, graphical interfacing with links to off-site sources, and user demands for quick off-blog references. In addition, the emerging common format for blogs found at hosting sites like Blogger, Movable Type, and JotSpot encourages a shared language and graphical interface for users that must be learned before one can be a proficient blogger.

These similar formats not only construct a genre, they contribute to the ease with which blogs mass-distribute information. On the Internet, a blog becomes immediately visible and searchable. Readerships can develop quickly, as does mimetic thought. Memes, little phrases or words that travel and replicate throughout culture like a virus, spread rapidly and enter our daily lives. Mass media once provided the dispersion of mimetic thoughts, ideas, or slogans, but these days memes spring eternal from blog sites.

For educators and parents, this information reformation creates a different sort of digital divide. To the uninitiated or under-initiated, the information presented in a blog seems more style than substance, devoid of genuine content, a place where tightly packed jargon and loosely constructed opinions dominate. In some instances, teachers' and parents' perceptions might be right. However, to paint all blogs with such a broad brush diminishes the effect they have on integrating pleasure, play, and the pursuit of information in learning. Blogs have a place in education. But for blogs to really take hold as an educational activity that has merit, educators and parents have to consider how to incorporate them into America's classrooms.

They Are a Malleable Writing Genre

Bloggers teach us that information and knowledge are not static items. Moreover, these same bloggers show us that a blog is a pliable writing genre, one that can be adapted to a variety of online occasions, purposes, and situations. These are important lessons to learn if educators and parents want to prepare their children for communicating in a global society now dominated by multimedia technologies, an overwhelming influx of raw information and visual images, and a networked economy.

While the next chapter addresses literacy issues related to blogging in greater depth, it is important to know that a blog can fluidly adapt to both the aesthetic and the grammatical aspects of writing. For educators this is crucial, as a blog adjusts to student writers' progress and development. For parents, understanding that a blog can conform to their children's intellectual and emotional development helps many adults realize that blogging helps their children make sense of complex feelings, issues, or concerns that affect their lives both in school and at home.

As students must adhere to certain stylistic, rhetorical, or mechanical conventions in classroom settings, on their blogs they can practice these skills and strategies in a real-world writing context. If the blogs are made public, then genuine feedback from external readers can provide another dimension of formative assessment. If the blogs are kept private through password protection or specific K–12 restrictions, then students still have the opportunity to play with written language and receive good feedback from peers. This too can be beneficial for assessment, especially with younger student writers. Feedback is an extremely important component of keeping younger writers focused on the writing process.

With public blogs, parents can surf the blogosphere and monitor their children's behavior. While some kids are sophisticated enough to place elements of their blog off-limits to all but select friends, parents are usually able to access the information. Adolescents who maintain risqué blogs frequently do so because they realize their parents have no knowledge of the blogosphere. Parents with some comprehension of the potential for blogs as a learning tool can steer their children away from displaying personal or provocative information and move them toward using blogs in ways that build strong literacy skills and work in tandem with school lessons.

Both teachers and parents need to realize this crucial point in adolescent blogging: Whether the blogs are public or private, students are learning how to balance information to fit to online spaces and audi-ences' needs as well as a writer's personal interests. This is an important phase in becoming digitally literate. Blogs conform to a multitude of visual and aural rhetorical practices in their ability to layer in graphics, audioblogging, and now videoblogging. So bloggers must learn to inte-grate visual, aural, and verbal skills. All this contributes to the honing of multiple intelligences, an issue taken up in greater length later in this book, in preparation for life and learning in a global society.

Perhaps the best aspect of blogs as a malleable genre is the ability to address voice in writing. Put simply, voice is the writer's selection of words, tone, rhythm, sentence structure, and arrangement to put for-ward personality or identity on the page. The blog format encourages the creation of a writer's persona, the play of words, sentences, and identity enhanced by color, graphics, links, music, and sound. On a blog, a shy child can become emboldened and an athlete can display her in-tellectual side. Similarly, an honors student can express his "gangsta" side and the kid who appears to be a delinquent can show his concern for humanity. What teachers, professors, and parents soon discover, if they visit students' blogs, is that the genre encourages students to be-come more than the one-dimensional people we see in our classrooms and homes.

They Allow Writers to Generate New Personas and Construct New Worlds

As I wrote this chapter, the Indianapolis Colts football coach Tony Dungy learned that his eighteen-year-old son, James, had committed suicide. By all media accounts, James Dungy was a mild-mannered, well-liked, Christian teenager from a very good family. However, the local Florida paper that covered the suicide noted that young Dungy had a blog on MySpace, a popular blog site for teenagers (Stroud, Gra-ham, Zayas, & Thompson, 2005). James Dungy's MySpace account por-trayed a different young man, one with a violent side that stood in stark contrast to the pleasant community college student his family and friends knew.

Not too long before Dungy's suicide, a fourteen-year-old girl, Kara Borden, of Lititz, Pennsylvania, saw her parents murdered by her boyfriend, David Ludwig, because they disapproved of her seeing the eigh-teen-year-old, whom she knew through home-schooling and church. Both Kara and the young man had blogs on Xanga and MySpace; Kara portrayed herself on Xanga as a seventeen-year-old who loved Jesus and partying and who thought "books are gay" (karebear00.Xanga.com), while on his blog, David spoke of his love for guns, hunting, and getting into trouble.

Earlier, in the summer of 2005, the blogosphere buzzed about Zach Stark's blog entries on MySpace. The Tennessee teenager, who is gay, announced to bloggers everywhere that his parents were forcibly send-ing him to Camp Refuge, a religious compound run by the group Love in Action, known for "rehabilitating" homosexuals. Zach's daily entries touched the lives of bloggers and gay rights activists around the country. The ensuing blog storm resulted in a federal judge upholding the state of Tennessee's prosecution of Love in Action for running a mental health facility without a proper license (Hunter, 2005).

The issue here is not whether MySpace, LiveJournal, or Xanga should be banned, nor is it that children involved in blogging are in emotional trouble. Blogs were not the reason behind any of these tragic events, and technology should not be blamed for the suicide and double mur-der. The issue is how adolescents and others use blogs to create new personae, new identities, dramatically different from the ones friends and family members know or want to see. My reason for including these three recent events is to underscore the importance of learning why stu-dents generate new worlds and personalities. While this idea is taken up at greater length later in this book, following are a few central points for background for these future chapters.

Adolescents try on new identities as they move into adulthood. Teen-agers' changing and forging of identities are incredibly important for their maturation, even though the process is trying and demanding on those around them. Adolescence is a complex time filled with contradic-tions, conflicts, desires, hopes, and insecurities. Blogs become an open diary of sorts, a place where we can read and watch these personalities and identities change. Partly confessional, partly braggadocio, partly cool poses, partly a front for becoming the person a child thinks he or she is, blogs are a study in teenage narcissism.

In some ways, blogs are a teenage way of playing dress-up: like little children who dip into Mom's makeup and Dad's closet, then parade around the house in adult finery, adolescent bloggers frequently find themselves with one foot in childhood and one in adulthood. Unlike little kids in their parents' clothes, however, blogs are more than a snapshot in time. Blogs remain even after the child has both figuratively and literally gone.

This is why teachers, professors, administrators, and parents often find themselves at a loss to explain the sometimes dramatic changes they discover between the child in front of them and the person blogging on the screen. What adults need to realize is that preteens and adolescents use blogs, like text messages on cell phones or wikis or whatever the latest communication model is, to gain recognition, find others with shared interests, and develop a sense of solidarity among others. Students use MySpace, Bebo, Blogger, Xanga, and other blog sites as a way to meet friends and build social relationships. Rather than engage in socially awkward face-to-face communication, tweenage and teenage bloggers use the blogosphere's anonymity to generate a personality they think will impress others.

Because blogs are flexible enough to conform to whatever voice, personality, or identity a child or a teenager wants, students can have a number of blogs to represent their various personality dimensions. Quite often, these representations are alternatives to the everyday images teachers and parents see. In addition, the worlds our tweenage and teenage bloggers create are frequently far different from the ones in which they live. Not necessarily fantasy worlds, these blog worlds illustrate aspects of multiple dispositions, qualities, and outlooks that are part of the young blogger's self. Blogs become a way for many self-conscious teenagers and late adolescents to network and create a new world where they seem more suave and sophisticated—contrasted to their real-life feelings of clumsiness, klutziness, inelegance, and gracelessness.

Blogs do not create the social problems that generated James Dungy's suicide, the Borden family double murder, or Zach Stark's "treatment" for being a gay teen. Nor do blogs create the complex real worlds these and other teenagers inhabit. Those social problems and adjustment complications existed long before blogs emerged, and they will remain long after blogs turn into something else. But blogs provide adults with an insight into how preteens, teens, and college students negotiate the complexities of their home and school lives.

With 2005 WiredSafety.org estimates of more than six million kids blogging and the numbers of new-kid blogs rising each month, educators and parents need to learn more about why their students and children are blogging. Shutting down blog hosting sites for preteens, teenagers, and college students is not the answer. For most tweens and teens, blogging is a way to forge independent personalities, create solidarity with others who share similar interests, and generate that "teenage space" where they can grow and become responsible citizens and netizens. As the next section will show, having that public space where writers can raise their voices when they feel marginalized in real life is very important.

They Empower Those Who Are Often Marginalized

Writers never underestimate the power of voice in writing. Voice is the collective effect of a writer's use of language on a reader. Writers can encourage the development of their written voice by finding avenues where they can tell their stories.

Storytelling is an important feature of building a writer's voice. When we tell stories, our authentic voice emerges. Not an academic voice, a voice that often strains against rules of objectivity and propriety. Not a neutral voice, where writers try to distance themselves from a situation. But an authentic voice, one in which writers attempt to blend concrete facts and vivid details with comfortable diction to fit their audience.

Because their history is drawn from the epistolary (letter-writing) and diary genres, blogs encourage storytelling. This same foundation is also what encourages confessional writing, diary entries, and many other blog-like missives. Storytelling keeps historical or cultural events, personal moments, and missing or missed individuals alive and present in another's life. So stories about a teenager's daily life, a young soldier's harrowing experiences in a foreign land, or a child's perception of a parent's unfamiliar but scary disease each provide both an outlet for emotional release and a conduit to keep memories of another person, place, or event alive.

The Pew Internet study on blogs conducted in 2005 (Lenhart, Madden, & Hitlin 2005; Rainie, 2004) suggests that minorities, women, and teenagers are entering the blogosphere in record numbers. It is no coincidence that these social groups have often been on the periphery of mainstream society. When people are, or feel that they are, marginalized, their voices are denied. If society refuses to listen to their stories, these individuals will eventually find an outlet where their voices can be heard. With tweens and teens, teachers and parents should strive to find those places where youngsters' voices can be expressed in a constructive, rather than destructive, way.

Blogs, because they tap into adolescents' social relationships, can become a practical and useful medium for helping youngsters express their voices in the world. Blogs offer a voice to those who have been or who have felt marginalized in mainstream society because of their race, age, economic status, political views, gender, or health. They are a productive way to let students articulate their views about the world around them.

When teachers and parents encourage their students or children to blog, they are furthering young writers' opportunities to tell their stories, to give voice to the full range of their emotions, beliefs, and concerns. By supporting young writers' adventures in blogging, teachers and parents show confidence in students' abilities to find the stories they want to tell to others. Such reinforcement advances literacy skills and promotes independent learning.

The stories of tweens and teens who use blogs inappropriately for sex, to commit crimes, or to lash out violently at themselves or at others are telling society, their teachers, and their parents a particular story. These are stories most of us do not want to hear, as the narratives are filled with pain, frustration, anger, and hate.

Again, blogs are not the cause of these stories. They are simply the venues where the narratives are told and retold. Teachers, professors, and parents can intervene in these narratives, sometimes just by reading the blogs and commenting on them. When stories of pain, hate, anger, and sadness come forth, all of us must realize that whether they are fronts for some persona or are indicative of genuine distress, the voices that tell these stories have been or feel marginalized in their worlds.

WHY DO STUDENTS BLOG?

From sensationalized media reports to in-depth research studies, the evidence shows that students are blogging in record numbers. That fact doesn't seem like it will change for the foreseeable future. So why do students blog? In a nutshell, most students blog because they want to be recognized, to have their stories heard in a complex world that really doesn't seem to listen. Students blog because it's fun; through their blogs they meet others who have shared interests and they form communities without the social awkwardness of meeting face-to-face. Students blog because they want to belong somewhere, anywhere, where people care about them. Whether in the library, a dorm room, a homeroom, a campus coffee shop, or a dining room, students blog because they want to be loved and respected for who they are and what they think. In that respect, they follow a long tradition held by writers: They want to express themselves and provoke ideas using the written word for a large audience. In short, students blog because they want their voices to be heard and they want to feel connected to others.

2

BLOGGING AND NEW LITERACIES

Writing takes center stage in the new media environment resulting from the Internet's development. It is, without question, a core skill for bloggers. Proficient bloggers must be adept at both writing and critiquing the English language in order to reach their desired audience.

Even so, writing for blogs requires users to maintain a special sort of literacy, different than what is learned in the classroom. Blog writing, in the form of producing highly readable online text, offers a very different take on traditional literacy taught in schools. Traditional education stresses reading over writing and is tied to alphabetic literacy, a standard in American schools since the 19th century. Literacy as it had been defined for more than a century has always been "reading and writing," with writing coming second.

With the Internet explosion in the late 20th century and the incredible growth of e-mail and chat rooms, writing has commandeered a prominent place in online communication. But writing is supplanted with visual images and sound in most electronic communication, and whether that imagery includes color, music, graphics, or font changes depends on the writer's skill and needs. If a writer cannot write in the modes appropriate for the electronic universe, he or she will be marginalized—considered "information illiterate" by those around the writer. As cyberspace has transformed into the blogosphere, writing's prominence has been solidified as a necessary literacy skill. But these days writing in the blogosphere differs from the type of student writing prepared for marbled-covered composition notebooks.

Once upon a time, neat penmanship and crisp pages were goals for work presented to teachers. Readability became defined by a writer's legible script, and literacy was expressed through vocabulary and connections between the writer's words and how well those words matched class readings. In the blogosphere, writing and its connection to visual images, sound, and color are used carefully to lead audiences in reading texts. Handwriting is of minimal or no concern. Correct keyboarding is crucial.

Bloggers arrange written information along with images, colors, sounds, and links to direct readers' attention. They take a highly active role in the production of texts and the distribution of information compared to writers in the past. Literate bloggers are aware of how to best select, evaluate, and manipulate information for an audience, as well as which media (sound, fonts, color, images, or graphics) to choose in order to highlight important data. Precise keyboarding is necessary to ensure the underlying code is correct so that links work, colors are appropriate, and graphics load properly.

Writing is elevated to a core skill in the blogosphere, but teachers, professors, and parents must realize that in this "new literacy" writing emerges as only *one* part of a communicated message. It is certainly true that literate bloggers have to have strong storytelling skills, excellent syntactic and organizational abilities in presenting information, and a vigorous writing style to convey the content. However, highly literate bloggers also develop an aesthetic sense of arranging the content in visually attractive, easily understood (or "chunked") units. Highly literate bloggers recognize that this new medium demands writing in terms of design, not just expression.

Bloggers also have to make a number of decisions related to the writing process that they would not have had to make in a paper-based writing environment. For instance, they have to determine whether the audience better understands the content presented as written text, as a visual image, as a sound, or as a link to an off-site article, essay, or text. This step alone requires that bloggers think differently about the material in front of them. On a blog, clear, concise writing alone will not necessarily convey the right message.

As a result, literacy is a much broader set of practices when writers blog. The shift in literacy practices arises because of the blog's public element. Bloggers actively engage in making meaning for others. Bloggers make judgments about what information is presented, as well as *how* it is presented. Because messages are meant for a public readership, bloggers also have to consider the social, cultural, emotional, and political dimensions of their words and the extent to which those components will shape a reader's response.

Many writing teachers will argue that these points are similar to what they expect in a paper-based writing assignment, but if those teachers were being honest they would note that, with rare exception, students pay little attention to these factors in their classroom tasks. This is because most classroom writing is private or semiprivate in nature, with only the teacher and possibly a handful of peers reviewing the work. Deft student writers might be able to fool a teacher or peer group with style or verbal facility, but in the blogosphere, sharp readers with access to the facts can make clever students look inane or immature. Since most adolescents avoid the potential for public embarrassment, teenage blog writers tend to spend more time and care when their words are being uploaded to the world.

Perhaps the greatest shift in literacy and writing wrought by blogs is that students rather than their instructors now have control of the learning and writing process. With blogs, students can write anywhere and at any time; no teachers are required to lead the activity. Student writers can increase their knowledge and communicate with dozens, if not hundreds, of other similar thinkers. It is as if composition theorist Peter Elbow's 1973 words have come true—bloggers are now "writing without teachers."

Because students are writing without teachers, they can follow their passions in writing and direct their own learning beyond the classroom. Whether students find genetics or the Spanish artist Francisco de Goya fascinating, they can build a blog around that excitement and teach the world. This has far more relevance as a learning tool than writing a five-, ten-, or fifteen-page paper on the topic, as the finished blog can encourage other experts or aficionados to respond to the students' efforts. Writing in a real-world situation like a blog generates student writers' enthusiasm, not just for the topic at hand but for writing as well.

USING BLOGS TO BUILD LITERACY IN THE CLASSROOM

Teachers and professors who use blogs in the classroom to build student literacies often tell stories about how their classes respond eagerly to blogging activities. Like many others, I too have found that over time and with practice my students become willing and engaged participants in the blogging process. This corresponds to four points made generally about the intersections of pedagogy and digital technology:

1. Blogging encourages fluency in writing.
2. Blogging encourages cooperative learning.
3. Blogging encourages critical thinking.
4. Blogging encourages performance-based learning (PBL) among other cross-curricular strategies.

Taking each of these points, let's examine how blogging affects literacy.

It Encourages Fluency in Writing

Blogging encourages fluency in writing for two straightforward reasons: First, as noted in the first chapter, it is a pleasurable activity. Because student writers view blogging not as academic writing but as external to schooling, writing emerges as a "fun" activity. Second, students frequently spend more time on their blogging tasks than on other school-based writing assignments because of the hands-on, self-directed, gratifying autotelic aspects of working on a blog. The rewards of blogging come from building something that has immediate, tangible feedback. Writers can see a published document almost instantaneously, and they long for commentary to acknowledge their efforts. When writers find the act of writing enjoyable and satisfying, they tend to write longer and with more care.

It Encourages Cooperative Learning

Cooperative learning, as most educators and some parents know, describes situations in which students work together to complete a set task or series of tasks. Depending on the grade level and subject taught, cooperative learning is either flexible or structured, based on the instructor's or the curriculum's desired outcome. In many school settings, cooperative learning brings together students of diverse backgrounds or multiple intelligences, encourages prosocial behaviors and values among students, fosters higher-level reasoning, and deepens cognitive development. In college-level courses, cooperative learning promotes the understanding of other perspectives, simulates professional work environments, and deepens the transfer of learned knowledge.

Blogging encourages cooperative learning through the feedback loop. As students post to others' sites, a form of collective intelligence develops about a topic. In the blogosphere, this commonly circulated knowledge or information is continually improved or bettered as it is shared, usually resulting in the successful assembly of new skills and practices.

Students generate collective intelligence and future skills through cooperative action when they write on blogs. They learn to read, write, analyze, and evaluate the information in front of them, with the intent of discovering more. Through cooperative learning spaces like blogs, students find out that no single person knows everything and that shared inquiry helps everyone uncover more useful information and knowledge.

As a cooperative learning activity, blogging teaches students that writers depend on readers, and readers on writers. One's performance as a writer or reader is often mutually grounded in the abilities of the other. Since communication requires a sender and a receiver—or with a blog, a writer and a reader—students begin to develop the sense that careful writers need to build a relationship with their readers to ensure that a message is understood.

It Encourages Critical Thinking

Cooperative learning through blogs spurs students' critical thinking. Because students have to discern the information they unearth about a topic and then write about it using language so others can understand, student bloggers have to learn how to ask good questions in order to evaluate information or to become better researchers in order to make certain assessments. Mere writing style is not enough to sway savvy outside readers; student writers need to be certain of their facts and data to support the ideas they hope to present in a public forum.

Consequently, blogging helps students sharpen their persuasive and argumentative writing skills. As student bloggers gather their research and select the information to present, a clear position emerges on the topic. Because blogs encourage writing from a first-person perspective ("I," either clearly expressed or implied), students have to take a stand. Then, to support this view, student bloggers must generate links to supporting materials, offer challenges to others' comments or data, and refute countering positions or information. During this process, the research they conduct expands their knowledge and background on various academic subjects.

It Encourages Cross-Curricular Learning and Writing Strategies

For the reasons listed previously, blogging complements performance-based learning (PBL), writing across the curriculum (WAC), and other cross-curricular learning initiatives. Student writers creating a blog satisfy the "performance" element of PBL. The hands-on approach to building one's own writing environment teaches students to write by generating the very situation in which they *will* write. Conversely, the traditional method for teaching writing is to have the teacher or professor stand in front of the room, hand out a prompt, and ask students to respond in prose. While writing pedagogy argues that student writers should develop some portable or transferable skills, practicing writing to a prompt or in response to reading does little to encourage writers' skill transference.

Because a blog is a personalized learning environment in a real setting, it simulates a genuine writing activity. Student writers learn about writing by completing a real writing task. In many ways, the blog becomes an interactive teacher. As students build their blogs and create their content, they have to respond to questions the blog site manager asks during the construction and development of their blog. Once the site is up and running, students then have to consider what pieces of information and visual references are needed to keep readers' attention. This process emulates the expectations and demands real writers face.

A cornerstone of most writing-across-the-curriculum programs in schools, colleges, and universities is writing to learn. Instead of writing for a particular purpose, such as to inform, to persuade, or to entertain, students write in order to "think on paper." Or, as is the case with blogs, students "think online." With writing to learn, students write to discover more about key concepts and subject material rather than to demonstrate mastery. Using disciplinary or subject areas, students can use their blogs as a way to support or reject expert opinion in published journals, explore the use of jargon in a particular profession, or compose journal entries to clarify difficult class readings or lectures. If blogs are used as a writing-to-learn strategy, students will be exposed to inductive learning and they will become more comfortable conducting self-directed inquiry. Again, such learning supports the intent behind teaching critical thinking in schools.

What educators and parents soon learn is that blogging can be completed in any class and at almost any grade level, in school or college. Because students generally take pride in their blogs, as they are meant for public view, instructors, administrators, and parents do not have to be grammar police. Students will rise to the expectation that grammar matters in their blog writing. No one, especially a high school student, wants to be embarrassed by an anonymous post, in a public venue, correcting typos and poor syntax. As a result, students will take responsibility for editing and proofing their writing.

BLOGGING AND SPECIAL-NEEDS STUDENTS

America's philosophy toward education has historically been that all students have the right to a free and appropriate education. In the 21st century, an appropriate education includes using technology to build literacy skills. For a significant segment of our student population, this right is frequently denied because of educators', administrators', and parents' lack of knowledge regarding assistive computer technology. Free or relatively inexpensive software tools like blogs can improve the lagging literacies of special-needs students, and understanding how blogging can assist in developing special-needs students' literacies is crucial if educators and parents hope to ensure the undeniable right for American students to have the education they deserve.

While blogging helps most students develop broad-based literacy skills, it might actually be a greater benefit to certain groups of special-needs students. For deaf, visually impaired, at-risk, emotionally challenged, and ESL/ELL students in particular, blogging offers an opportunity for expression in learning environments that are not always kind or encouraging. These students can benefit greatly from the blogging experience, as external audiences often provide a sense of community that school communities frequently do not present to them.

Here is a brief story I often tell to illustrate the point I'm trying to make: A few years ago, one of my graduate students who then worked in medical publishing, Leigh Kobert, explained the value of digital literacies for those who are either learning-challenged or disabled. Leigh suggested that for these individuals, students or not, the "body-less" quality of electronic communication provided the ability to communicate to those who might not have the physical capability to engage in oral or written conversations. To illustrate, she recalled a series of e-mail exchanges she had with coworkers who had physical and learning disabilities. Leigh's coworkers found that e-mail, like other asynchronous communication, took away the prejudices and perceptions they had to deal with otherwise.

Leigh proposed that blogs are a way for writers to be treated the ways they have always wanted to be viewed, as thinkers and transmitters of ideas and feelings. Blogs become locations where mentally or physically challenged students can exist without being judged or labeled by their disabilities. Leigh's view was that electronic modes of communication and expression like e-mail and blogs allow writers to be evaluated outside the shell of a limited body, the frustration of language or restricted speech and hearing, and the challenge of complex analytical thought. Leigh's point has resonated with me ever since.

If teachers and parents consider the stigma of students being labeled "emotionally disturbed," "an English-language learner," a "second-language learner," or "at risk," it becomes easier to see why "body-less" communication through blogs might encourage a large segment of student writers to express themselves. For students who find their bodies to be a trap, either because of physical disability, obesity, or adolescence, the ability to separate their voices from their bodies must be a liberating moment. On a blog, students who traditionally would not be heard or who are dismissed by a label can join a community that values them as thinking, feeling human beings. Being able to give voice to a range of ideas, feelings, and perceptions opens these students to new worlds of literacies that might be closed to them in traditional or main-stream classrooms.

BLOGGING AND DEAF STUDENTS: A WAY TO HEAR THEIR WORDS

An overlooked area in blogging pedagogy, as with other pedagogical issues, particularly in higher education, is that of deaf students. While some students might want to audioblog, sound is not a necessary component for blog writing, so deaf students can maintain blogs in order to communicate more easily with others.

In an era when federal school mandates, state standards, and assessment tests require hearing-impaired students to perform at the same level as their hearing-intact peers, a method needs to be in place for teaching writing to those students who have never heard words or sentences. Blogs can be that method.

For students who are isolated from their classmates because of hearing loss, blogs are way to form social relationships with peers while practicing writing skills. Blogging is a way for these students to develop a voice. Hearing-impaired students can overcome the lack of a spoken voice by creating a literary style that engages readers. They can also use their talents as keen observers to write with insight, reflection, and intuition about the daily events that surround them. Such entries build the type of writing skills necessary for a student to become a proficient writer. Moreover, these are the characteristics that make both writers and bloggers cherished by their audiences.

BLOGGING AND VISUALLY IMPAIRED STUDENTS

Educators and parents who interact with visually impaired students might wonder how blogging can benefit these young writers. Through audioblogging technology, podcasts, and screen readers, visually impaired student writers can also contribute to the blogosphere. Access to these adaptive technologies is often provided free or at a reasonable price for students and their parents. A simple Google search for "audioblogging" can lead to a range of available software and shareware options.

Audioblogs usually have a title and a dated entry like other blogs, but the bulk of the content is delivered through sound. The editorial content of audioblogs is frequently combined with sound and links, so all visitors can participate. Audioblogging encourages visually impaired students to interact with their sighted peers, and so helps these students feel part of the classroom community. Audioblogging is very simple, and most blog hosting sites have free audioblog software packages to assist writers. They can usually be developed via MP3 or MP4 files, podcasts, or audiofeeds. In many ways, audioblogs, podcasts, and audiofeeds parallel radio broadcasts. Writers produce content that appears in print, linked, and aural forms. Students who audioblog develop a range of important new literacy skills that connect them to the Information Age, so teachers and parents should encourage visually impaired students to use audioblogs in their writing. Blogs allow a large number of students to respond to these young writers and a range of feedback mechanisms to support their writing efforts.

What is especially exciting for visually impaired students is that audioblogging lets them participate in the same activities as mainstreamed students, and even be slightly ahead of the technological curve by using audiofeeds or podcasts to produce their blogs. Such advancements help special-needs students build self-esteem and confidence, especially when they receive feedback from classmates and others. As visually impaired students become comfortable with audioblogging, they can then move toward writing more traditional blogs using Braille keyboards and screen readers. Over time and with a bit of practice, visually impaired students can participate in creative, engaging writing activities with their classmates.

BLOGGING AND EMOTIONALLY CHALLENGED OR AT-RISK STUDENTS

Students who are categorized as emotionally disturbed or at risk share a similar characteristic: They tend to be socially isolated. Labeling students in either manner often increases the separation. Blogging can be used to overcome the loneliness and seclusion these students often feel in classroom settings.

Many times students who are considered emotionally challenged or at risk display highly creative, sensitive, and intuitive behaviors. Blogs can nurture these characteristics, as students' postings combine the individuals' thoughts and feelings with an interactive writing environment. Teachers and parents can cultivate students' creativity by supporting these writers' integration of graphics, sound, color, and video to express the range of emotions and ideas these adolescents hold inside. Because blogs use multiple formats to present content, these writers can blend conventions, cultural or symbolic images and meanings, and traditional language to tap into alternatives for creating meaning and knowledge in the classroom. For at-risk students especially, a blog's fluidity in blending formats and conventions might mesh better with their own learning styles, and the blog can bridge the students' current literacy practices and the school's expectations for academic literacy.

Certain student writers are more comfortable seeing the connection between and among ideas rather than internalizing decontextualized facts. Many times at-risk and emotionally challenged learners are, at their core, discovery learners. Such students learn and retain concepts better when they discover the material on their own rather than passively listening to a lecture or taking notes. In those instances, blogging incorporates self-directed inquiry, which often furthers discovery learning.

While learning in a style that more closely matches their own, these students also increase their digital and information literacy by practicing keyboarding, Internet searching, file management, and software usage. These real-world skills resonate with emotionally disturbed and at-risk students. First, they are hands-on, and students have a sense of accomplishment when a task is completed. Second, digital and information literacies seem more relevant to the interests and expectations these students have for schooling. While the classics of English and American literature often seem removed from these students, creating and maintaining a blog that reaches out to the world is concrete and achievable. Third, students can work at their own pace—speeding up or slowing down in relation to their ability to grasp new material and process it for a genuine audience.

If educators' and parents' purpose in sending students to school is to provide them with an appropriate learning experience, then learning how to blog can be a great way to develop written literacy. For all the reasons listed earlier in this section, blogging can be particularly useful for students resistant to traditional literacy practices like book reading and essay writing.

BLOGGING AND ENGLISH-LANGUAGE LEARNERS

Perhaps the most research in blogging with special-needs students is in relation to English-language learners. The conversational aspect of blogging encourages second-language learners to practice their idiomatic English. And because blogs are a print-based medium, English-language learners can also focus on honing their reading skills. If audioblogging or podcasting is included in the classroom blogging experience, then these students will be able to work on their spoken English as well.

Whether educators consider having a class blog to hold group conversations or establishing individual blogs where students can free-write as a discovery writing strategy, the use of blogs in an ESL classroom is a great idea for teaching fluency, idiomatic or conversational discourse, and cultural or social exchanges in conversation. Since many English-language learners are hesitant to participating in conversations or resistant to sharing their writing with native speakers, a blog can be a place to practice together and form a community before venturing into more mainstreamed language activities.

These students bring a diverse perspective to classroom blogs—one that is sometimes lost in traditional daily classroom routines. English-language learners frequently have rich experiences outside of school, and they can teach mainstream students much about the world. When English-language learners tell their stories, they not only feel ownership over the learning experience because they are sharing new information, but they also become part of the larger classroom and cultural fabric. Through blogging, these students can participate in the school community.

BUILDING LITERACIES IN ALL STUDENTS

Although the previous section concerned special-needs students and blogging, all students can build valuable new literacy skills through blogging. Blogging advances learning through the "zone of proximal development," a theory developed well over one hundred years ago by Russian cognitive psychologist Lev Vygotsky.

Vygotsky defined the zone of proximal development as that area in which students can perform tasks both with and without the assistance of a teacher, parent, or peer. With the ease of current blogging technology, teachers and parents can create a base from which students can grow and develop with minimal support. When introducing the concept of blogging, teachers and parents can model the behaviors they hope to see in the students, then gradually pull back and let students move forward on their own. Left to their own devices, students will begin to solve problems through reasoning and conversation, both written and oral. At this stage, students enter the zone of proximal development where their cognitive, linguistic, and technical processes start to mature.

Independent student learning can be advanced through blogging, as students create the topics and threads for discussion, either under guidance or as free-writing. An important step in Vygotsky's theory is eventually for students to teach others. With blogging, this step is attainable. Since blogs are public or semipublic, students can teach their classmates regardless of whether they are mainstreamed or labeled as special-needs.

Multiple levels of cooperative learning also happen at this stage because students who are technologically proficient can be paired with those who struggle; similarly, artistic or graphically inclined students can work with advanced writers. But students must also work alone to complete blog tasks or in tandem with software directions and manuals. Then at some point students network their blogs, and other users join together in a feedback or commentary process. This offers a social dimension that promotes student reflection, thinking, and expression through language.

Consequently, collaborative or cooperative learning becomes a much more well-rounded process, which leads to mastery. Students not only begin to take ownership of their blogs, they begin mastering their information literacy and traditional literacy skills because they can take over the instructor's role. Their ideas become fuller and richer because of the social interaction of other writers, who challenge or question posted thoughts.

Blogging is such an effective instructional tool because it is a hands-on activity, is set in various learning contexts, and addresses cultural diversity in collaborative, community-based practices. Through blogging, students learn how to learn according to their own needs and rhythms.

Because the concept of "literacy" is changing in light of technology's rapid pace, there is much that educators, administrators, and parents still need to learn to help students gain the education they need in order to be productive, active citizens. Regardless of how literacy is ultimately defined, students must be shown how to learn about learning so they can adapt to cultural and societal shifts in information and knowledge gathering.

Blogging represents one of the early moves in broadening literacy as a reaction to cultural and societal change. In the blogosphere, one's physical ability or appearance matters less than what one thinks, feels, and perceives. Moreover, information, knowledge, content, and meaning are context- rather than authority-driven. This swing requires students to become less dependent on teachers and parents for their learning experience.

With literacy's expansion and the technological resources to ensure that all students can participate in learning, the instructional role of educators and parents also shifts. Rather than seeing these authority figures as the sole basis of information, knowledge, and content, students can compare these resources with larger data and information pools. They then begin to take control of their learning, ensuring that, in combination with state-mandated studies, they expand their subject knowledge by identifying and collecting materials they find interesting, relevant, and significant—material they can share with the classroom and global community.

Through blogging, students can bridge cultural, economic, social, physical, emotional, technological, and geographic limitations to learning. As a result, a new form of pedagogical logic and practice has to be developed and presented to educators and parents to accommodate such an expansion of the learning process. While it seems most reasonable right now to ground such pedagogical shifts in Vygotsky's "zone of proximal development," other foundational theories must be developed to accommodate future electronic literacy activities.

In short, blogging might turn out to be the tipping point in education for lifelong learning. Its adaptive nature, malleability, and ease of use make blogs a killer application. Like its predecessor, e-mail, blogs might soon develop into a ubiquitous communication tool in schools. For literacy, this will be an important event: having an inexpensive, ever-present, easy-to-use method for transmitting information, knowledge, and meaning across student populations, suggesting that it is indeed possible to teach and upgrade the literacies students need right now and will continue to need in the future.

③

BLOGS AS A NEW WRITING GENRE

If literacy practices are shifting and expanding, as I suggest in both chapters 1 and 2, then writing must also be changing in the process. This makes sense, since at literacy's core writing exists as a parallel to reading and visual rhetoric. Writing and its attendant processes are altered in electronic communication, and even though we all are in the middle of these changes and might not always feel comfortable explaining why they occur, we certainly see the differences in spelling, punctuation, and grammar that now occur in online writing.

Whether educators and parents find these alternatives liberating or the downfall of civilization remains a point of discussion in contemporary society. Certainly this is not a discussion I want to pursue here, as the answers are wrapped up in political and ideological concerns that cannot be resolved within a few pages. The central issue for the discussion following this chapter is that blogging heralds a new form for writing and communicating ideas, resulting in more effective student learning. This, to me, seems a more constructive way to think about the linguistic variations that occur in students' writing processes when they blog.

First, though, we have to ask what it means to call blogs a "new" writing genre? How do blogs differ from other current and older forms of writing?

UNDERSTANDING *GENRE*

Before we can decide whether a blog is a "new" writing genre, I must explain what *genre* is. Simply, *genre* means form. A writing genre, then, means the form or shape that writing takes.

Typical writing genres are letters, poems, short stories, novels, reports, and newspaper articles. In school, additional writing genres are research and academic papers, plays, histories, and essays. Some writers are considered masters of a particular genre; for instance, Shakespeare is a masterful playwright and Toni Morrison is a brilliant poet. Some writers are skilled wordsmiths in a practical genre: An advertising copywriter or newspaper reporter is often regarded as being talented enough to earn a living through words.

Most writers, though, learn a variety of genres and perform well enough to communicate their ideas to others using one or two forms. Many feel comfortable writing in genres that are connected to their livelihood; when asked to step out of their comfort zone, they defer to others. That's not uncommon, but in the information age a good number of people are learning something new about the writing they have to do: It doesn't conform to anything any of them ever learned how to write.

E-mail and text messaging on cell phones blend conversation and stenographer-like shorthand with odd punctuation. These days, people write in acronyms and show their emotions with unusual combinations of punctuation and letters. The era of long, fluid sentences and paragraphs filled with polysyllabic words is over. Information in text and e-mail messages is arranged, or "chunked" into small units that are easy to scan or skim. This marks the most noticeable shift in the writing process as it moves from paper to pixel.

And then there are blogs. For a traditionally educated person, blogs, with links, graphics, sound, and all that shorthand, acronymic, and clipped language look like hieroglyphics rather than messages. On top of that, some blogs take on a diary appearance, others function more like newspaper articles, and yet others are just a set of links and comments. The volume of writers mixing genres and breaking grammatical and presentation rules in blogging is enough to make a grammarian or English lit major cry—or at least cringe. Undoubtedly, the language of blogs is enough to confuse educators and parents, as many wonder whatever happened to the written English language they learned not so long ago.

What people are seeing is the rise of a new genre of writing—a form that blends styles, strategies, and structures to express content. A skilled writer of this new genre has to learn not only the traditional rules and conventions for writing, but also the variants needed to reach out to diverse audiences.

Proficient blog writing depends on a writer honing a set of literacy skills that cross several genres and styles. A blogger must be part graphic designer and part technology guru as well, since writing in this new genre is not just text. In many ways, successful blog writers design their writing for effect. Bloggers design their writing for a purpose, for their readership, for the electronic medium and genre in which they are working, and for the sources the writers hope to use to illustrate their points.

THE SIX TRAITS OF BLOG WRITING

Understanding blogs as a new genre of writing, then, is more than thinking about a blog as a different form for displaying content. As writers move into blogging, they must be conscious of six elements that affect the quality of their written content:

- Emphasis
- Tone
- Consistency
- Repetition
- Information placement
- Color

Frequently, a failure to address one if not all of these six elements can constrain blog writing. Understanding how these traits function in blogging is necessary for young writers to improve their style as well as their content presentation. Blogs, as a particular genre, often display a specific look and feel that differs from other genres, so when introducing the idea of blogging to student writers, it is important to have them visit a number of blog sites to note the variations, depending on the target audience.

Even though these terms are common ones for English majors or writers, how the vocabulary is understood in a blog setting differs from the terms' usage in print-based contexts. Over time, teachers showing students how to implement these traits when blogging strengthens youngsters' written literacy. Students come to know when to identify the appropriate situations for using a certain style or technique, and they also learn alternative styles to address various audience needs.

My hope is that educators and parents can assist young writers in making better decisions regarding when to adopt a blogging style over an academic style. Many of the problems in student writing stem from an inability or inexperience in recognizing the audience's expectations. Students enjoy writing in the "texting mode" found in electronic communication, so they transfer that style—usually inappropriately—to their academic writing. Similarly, some students internalize the academic style to a degree that their online written work suffers by sounding stilted, and thus the content appears unnatural, pretentious, or wooden. To be competent writers for the 21st century, we have to become hybrids—those who can shift linguistic registers or styles to fit the audience's needs and expectations.

Emphasis refers to the placement or arrangement of information to gain the reader's attention. Because of the smaller size of a blog entry, emphasis is crucial. The writer as blogger has to pull in the audience almost immediately to ensure a short post will be read.

What information should a writer emphasize on a blog? Clearly, any pressing new material should be entered, as should interesting links to off-site websites, newspaper articles, graphics, or other information that supports the central topic or idea. Surely any item that seems relevant to the blogger's overall theme and audience's interest should be emphasized. Whatever the writer decides, the information should always contain pertinent, high-quality content and be well-written. Poor content and writing leads audiences to think the blogger has *blogorhea,* or producing a high volume of low-quality or irrelevant material. Sites labeled as being blogorhea tend to be ignored by most people.

Once writers develop their content and prose, they must pay attention to the placement of this information on the blog. Most online readers prefer a symmetrical style, with a balance between open space and text or images. An uncluttered blog site appears more inviting and restful for readers. If there are too many elements on the page, a hallmark of an unskilled blogger, readers' eyes have to dart and move too quickly to take in the necessary information. If an audience has to work too hard to gain desired information, then it will leave quickly or fail to return a second time. Neither is a good outcome.

To achieve both balance and emphasis, skilled bloggers use boldface fonts, catchy headlines and subheadings, and graphics to call attention to a new posting. Blog entries usually have a dateline or time marker as well as reverse postings, so the most current entries are placed at the top. Since most blogs have weekly or monthly archives, readers can be referred to earlier archived postings to acquire older information.

Fonts, headlines, subheads, graphics, date and time markers, and archives help the blogger place information in the easiest, most retrievable way possible for the reader. As with print-based writing, successful bloggers make the reading experience as simple as possible for the audience.

Balancing graphics, fonts, colors, text, and images on screen has not always been a trouble-free task. Unlike writing a paper for a class assignment, where software tools allow margins and fonts to be preset and graphics can be dropped into the text with ease, in the past bloggers had to learn how to program HTML (hypertext markup language) code. And today's advanced bloggers learn XML (Extensible Markup Language) or RSS (a more robust version of XML) code.

However, novice bloggers and their teachers do not have to learn how to code. With the advances in blogging software programs, writers can use predesigned templates to provide a shell that properly aligns the balance of empty space to text and graphics. Sometimes these templates provide designated archival headings, profile information, and user-friendly items such as calendars, clocks, and digital counters to personalize a blog. Knowing some HTML or RSS code is useful, as it gives the writer a bit more flexibility in personalizing a template or offers total creativity in designing one's own template. But novices can start blogging with no code experience whatsoever.

In fact, in the early stages of blogging, it might help younger writers to begin with a template, then learn whatever HTML or RSS code is needed later to layer in sound, links, news updates, and other items. Starting with a template allows the student writer to focus primarily on the writing and placement of information, which are the two central elements of successful blog sites. As students master writing content and balancing it within a template, then they can be encouraged to learn some HTML code, as it will contribute to their digital literacy.

While it is difficult to say exactly how bloggers should balance the information readers see on screen, here are three tips:

- Make sure the content is clearly written and fresh.
- Consider why the audience wants to visit the blog.
- Consider the context for the blog.

Top blog sites have clearly written prose that offers a fresh perspective. Well-trained bloggers always keep in mind why their audiences stop and visit (to gain new information, to be entertained, to read opinion, and so on). They write for a purpose. But it's equally important to consider the blog's context. Developing a blog for a class grade is very different from putting together a daily journal of teenage activities. Student writers must take into account what the expectations are for the blogging task and think about the standards of conduct required to meet the mental image a teacher, administrator, or parent has if the blog is for a school-based assignment.

People's expectations and standards vary widely, so there is no reason why teachers, school administrators, and parents can't discuss what they expect for blog use with youngsters. Such conversations are an opportunity to teach a wider understanding of emphasis and balance to young writers.

Very broadly speaking, tone is the emotional connection writers establish with their readers. Tone comes from the language and images bloggers use to present a subject to their audience. Emphasis and balance contribute to tone, as these elements can provide a sense of either harmony or chaos, calmness or movement, to the blog. Good blogging practices follow five very simple rules related to tone:

1. Keep the language and the content clean. A standard many bloggers use is that if Grandma would blush at what is said, then delete the line or change the wording.
2. Make sure the information presented is your own. Cite or link if not.

3. Don't disclose confidential or personal information, which can make you a target for stalkers, bullies, or other online predators.
4. Use a pen name to avoid unwanted correspondence.
5. Realize that once a post goes out, it cannot always be removed.

Great bloggers, like great writers, know that material can be presented without the use of "blue language." Part of the skill of blogging is how well you can use vocabulary. The creative use of language shows respect for readers. Educators and parents can show students examples from literature or elsewhere for inventing words or phrases to articulate certain thoughts.

My favorite authors for showing students how to generate humor, creativity, and respect for audiences include Chaucer, Shakespeare, Kurt Vonnegut, and Mark Twain. They write clearly and cleanly, and they inspire various tones in their work depending on the subjects they handle. Educators and parents can select their favorite authors, whether contemporary or classic, to show students their expectations for keeping the language respectable and acceptable for a wide readership. Working "blue" is useful for many talented stand-up comedians and can garner laughs, but for most professional contexts it's more reasonable to present a modest persona when online.

Besides keeping one's language in check, skilled bloggers ensure that whatever is posted is theirs alone. Many Internet users, especially younger students, believe that if something is online, it is fair game for appropriation without citation. That assumption is incorrect. Most Internet material is copyright-protected unless indicated somewhere on the website, and people who download and use the information as their own without permission or attribution are plagiarizing. Plagiarizing is academic fraud and can ruin a young student's future collegiate or professional career.

Another area where novice bloggers err is in the disclosure of private or confidential information. There are many reasons why students' school locations and names should never be made public, and these reasons parallel why workers should not reveal where they are employed. Beyond community embarrassment if in-house secrets are told, sometimes retaliation can occur. Retribution for blog commentaries can be quite vengeful, as has been seen in the business world, where people have been fired or denied tenure for what they posted on a blog. Regional newspapers are filled with stories of schools and school districts banning the student use of blogs because some naive blogger spreads rumors about classmates, teachers, administrators, or the school community. Later chapters in this book will address specific student-related concerns regarding why personal information should not be revealed on a blog site.

The Electronic Frontier Foundation, a watchdog group for Internet use, states clearly that bloggers do have first amendment rights to publish what they want. However, bloggers need to realize that they alone are responsible for the consequences of speaking their minds. The best rule for teaching students how to blog without reprisal is this: Don't publish secrets, but if you feel you must, use a pseudonym to protect yourself and your location.

Unless bloggers are well-known or public figures, most adopt a pseudonym or pen name. Using a pseudonym is a long-established practice in writing, as it protects the writer's identity. Authors use pen names whenever they feel their work is too risqué, upsetting to some readers, or too revealing of their real life and could expose innocent individuals.

A pen name provides a personality or a character that a blogger can use to write freely about a topic. It also encourages bloggers to write with an honest voice, or at least with a more vigorous voice and keener observations, than if they wrote under their real name. Sometimes, depending on the subject matter and content, a secret identity can protect bloggers from public or familial outrage.

For student writers, a pen name provides privacy from online predators or others who might cause harm. I encourage my students to use pseudonyms rather than their real names and locations because personal information should never be freely divulged on public space, given the issues surrounding identity theft and bullying or stalking. Savvy educators and parents should talk to student writers about these issues and encourage them to use an online name that differs from their given name.

Skilled bloggers understand the need to protect intellectual property, and they take great care in making sure borrowed information is cited. On a blog, there are many ways to cite a source. You can link directly to the source, creating a "permalink" (permanent link that archives the source material long after the blog's front page changes). Or you can take a snippet of the original text, highlight it on your blog, and then link to the source in case readers want more information. Lastly, you can simply provide citation material, either in an informal or formal manner, so viewers can search on their own for additional facts or data.

The last point about tone that student bloggers have to realize is that with some blogging software, once a post is sent it can't be deleted. This is why you should never blog when feeling angry, retaliatory, or vengeful. Many of the major blogging software packages now offer a way to remove a post, but all too often once something goes into the blogiverse the damage has been done. If possible, educators or parents should have the offending blogger delete or edit the post as quickly as possible and then explain why the redaction occurred.

However, some people never learn their lesson, whether in life or in the blogosphere. The best action to take if a young blogger continually violates the terms and conditions educators or parents set is to remove the offending blog from access by Google. This step is really a last resort, as it prevents people's right to access the blog. For those who are unfamiliar with this process, simply go to www.google.com/remove.html and then select the appropriate action. Educators or parents do not have to create a scene, run to the media with a press release, or initiate an in- or out-of-school suspension. All adults have to do is put the student in a blog "time out" of sorts. This sends a message that the misbehaving blogger's actions will not be tolerated without broadcasting the problem to the community.

Better ways to control abusive blogging exist than creating a huge to-do. Rather than posting to a blog in anger, student writers should be encouraged to find more constructive ways to handle their emotions before publishing hurtful, libelous, or slanderous comments. Remember, as society is learning these days about mean girls or violent boys, adults must take charge of the situation and bring about change, lest these abusive youngsters become abusive adults. A number of school-based social problems that spill over into blogs or the Internet can frequently be handled proactively if school leaders and parents talk to youngsters about appropriate tone and content for blogs before they begin their blogging experience. If this fails, then consequences should be meted out—like Google removal.

Student writers should learn the guidelines for enhanced blogging, as many experienced bloggers make snide or unfair comments about teenagers' blogs because they often violate the six rules presented earlier in the chapter. Tweens and teens are clearly not the only ones who err when blogging, but they have become stereotypes for poor blogging behaviors. There is no need to have students live up to these social stereotypes more than they already do.

WHY BLOGS ARE A NEW GENRE OF WRITING

Now that everyone has some background in understanding the basics of blog writing, it's time to explore why blogs are a new genre for writing. What makes the blog such a fascinating genre is that it is a composite of several genres, a blend of forms familiar to most of us. Part conversation, part diary, part narrative, part letter, part newspaper article, a blog performs diligently and reliably in whatever type of writing the blogger undertakes.

It is exactly this attribute that puts blogs into the "killer app" category as a genre. Killer applications change how people behave online. In what seemed to be a matter of months but was actually years, blogging has created a fascination in the written word—again—just as e-mail did almost twenty years ago and instant messaging has done in the past few years. Once again, because of blogs, it is cool to write.

Like e-mail, blogging is a cross-generational, cross-gender, and cross-ethnic endeavor. Also like e-mail, blogging is a socioeconomic class marker. Everyone can blog, as long as they have a computer and an access point. Scientists, media analysts, graduate students, stay-at-home parents, teenagers, lawyers, authors, publishers, truck drivers, nurses, soldiers, teachers, grandparents, and politicians all blog. Nowadays, we're finding that even kids in grade school blog. After major events like 9/11, the U.S. presidential election of 2004, and the 2005 Southeast Asian tsunami, the blogosphere was filled with the sound of a million people tapping on keyboards.

Still, in the process of reading others' blogs, most of us discover an important fact about blogging: Some writers blog well, and others blog inanely. As a trained writer and published author, I am all for the celebration of the written word. People becoming passionate about writing, and having their voices heard mirrors everything I believe to be important about the value of mastering language and literacy in a democratic society. But as a scholar, I also have to ask what blogs can do for writing that MOOspaces and hypertext and other electronic genres didn't do for many writers—why do blogs fill a technology gap in the teaching of writing and in the formation of literacy?

There are some early, plausible considerations for why blogs fill a technology gap. For example, blogs get writers back to the basics of the Internet. In an article by Bonnie Nardi, Diane Schiano, Michelle Gumbrecht, and Luke Swartz (2004), the authors note that blogging is "an interesting space within which the writerly craft is advanced." Nardi et al. explain that some writers' motivation for blogging comes from the thinking-writing connection. Those who use blogs in a think-write manner see their blogs as a muse.

The "blog as muse" is an apt metaphor. As an e-genre, blogs allow for a variety of written expressions in an easy-to-use format in which writers can concentrate on writing rather than technology. For scholarly or professional writers, a blog posting might be the germ of an idea that emerges later as a paper, essay, or larger project. For writers who dabble, a blog might be a place to offer up opinions or musings on everyday life. For schoolchildren, a blog can be a base for communicating with others, a way to develop a social network. But unlike other e-genres, a blog allows for feedback that enhances the writerly craft. In some instances, blogs become that ever-present conference where ideas are exchanged and refined—a think-write approach that encourages a thought to evolve into text.

Beyond the think-write approach, a blog's appeal is based on how well a writer can communicate with an audience. Blogs allow individuals to move from silence to articulating their voice without the need for extensive technical knowledge. Unlike a private journal, blogs provide a genuine audience—readers who are not always a part of one's immediate family and who respond to whatever is written. As a result, blogs encourage the expression of a personal voice in writing.

Lastly, and quite frankly, blogs are fun to create and tinker with over time. I really enjoy watching students sift through templates looking for that "perfect" blog skin (appearance) to best represent their personality, as well as the time they take and patience they show in setting up a blog or tearing it down when it doesn't seem "just right." In the ten years I've spent teaching writing through technology, I have yet to find the same sort of engagement that I see with my students and blogs. For me, observing students having fun with a blog reflects the incredible potential of blogs for everyone, students and adult learners alike. Teachers in the K–12 field tell me that this sense of pleasure and play in learning and writing extends into the middle and high school years, something that with more traditional teaching methods often dropped off after the primary grades.

From my perspective, the elements listed throughout this chapter are the main reasons why blogs have become a new writing genre. Bloggers can write as frequently as they want, in bursts of prose or in blocks of information. Moreover, blogs become an extension of writers' personalities and can be changed at whim or as the result of growth or changing circumstances. What viewers see is writers who are in the moment of writing, trying to capture how they are feeling and thinking at a particular point in time in relation to a topic.

As a killer application that has changed online behaviors toward writing and self-expression, blogs equal e-mail in terms of user-friendliness, adaptability, linguistic change, shifting rhetorical conventions, information dissemination, and democratic expression of ideas. Anyone who has access to a networked computer can blog, and with more people having some form of Internet entry through cell phones and PDAs, it makes sense that the number of bloggers increases each year.

Through these wireless and wired means, blogs show that students— regardless of age—have a deep interest in the written word. Students want to write, to share information, to research and read. But they want to do so on their own terms, not necessarily those that schools and colleges outline for them. What educators and parents must consider is how they can use blogs as a bridge between the student worlds and the academic or professional world inhabited by adults. Blogs are certainly malleable enough to become that link between school and the outside world; it is up to the grown-ups to figure out how to build those connections.

For blogs to become a killer app in education, instructors need to discover how the genre alters their students' writing behavior in the classroom. Blogs have to move away from being simply "interesting" or "clever," which marginalizes the genre. Most of the time, educators and parents think of blogs as a diversion or a game rather than a useful learning tool. Actually, blogs are a highly cost-efficient, accessible way to integrate writing instruction with information literacy across disciplines.

To move forward, instructors need to find appropriate avenues for incorporating blogs into writing pedagogy. Blogs can show students how to present the right information at the right time for the right audience using the right discourse strategies. Anne Davis, writing in the *eSchool News Ed-Tech Insider* newsletter (October 5, 2004), proposes several ideas for developing effective class blogs:

- Form online book groups where students respond to literature or readings.
- Create showcase portfolios where quality student work is displayed.
- Build a class newsletter.
- Link sections or classes to establish a writers' community.
- Establish a blog as a running evaluation of class activities and assignments.

Regardless of why they exist in the classroom, blogs can become a natural context for studying writing. This is something that has not happened with technologies such as hypertext or MOOspace. Nor has it happened with college "course-in-a-box" programs like WebCT or Blackboard.

Blogs often suffer the same fate as these other technologies in many writing classes. Blogs are often included as add-ons to the learning process because students think they are "cool" and it is relatively easy to motivate students to write in a blogging environment. Teachers allow students to blog because it seems more like entertainment than learning. For e-genres like blogs to take hold as a killer app in literacy or writing studies, instructors have to develop a different mind-set toward the process, one that addresses blogs as a method for delivering content rather than a way of playing with language.

Blogs do have the potential to emerge as a killer app in education. Teachers, parents, and students can see that their writing is being altered by the blogosphere, as are the ways in which we argue, persuade, manipulate, and disseminate information. What seems to be different for blogging compared to other technologies mentioned earlier is that the charge to write is not being led by the experts—that is, college writing faculties, renowned authors, and education professionals—but by students and laypeople.

Today's blog rush is more than a fad or a meme. If the 2005 Pew Internet study is correct, and we can only assume so because of the difficulty in capturing an actual number of blog users, then blogging is becoming part of the cultural mindset (Lenhart, Madden, & Hitlin, 2005). Blogging is changing the way people view writing, the writing process, and the finished product. It is indeed a new writing genre, one that has already altered our communication.

4

GENDER AND BLOGGING

Few bloggers would argue that the gender isn't a factor in the blogosphere. After all, gender is a factor in virtually every aspect of contemporary culture, blogging included. For a good number of us, however, the actual connection between gender and blogging is fuzzy at best. And few teachers and parents are clear as to the relationship among gender, blogging, and learning about writing. This chapter's focus centers on the links among gender, blogging, and student literacy, and what some readers discover about these linkages might be a surprise. With adolescents especially, gender plays an important role in blogging and developing information and technology literacies.

An overriding perception promoted by the mainstream media suggests that "kitchen table" issues like child care, education, health care, divorce, racism, sexism, and ageism are "girlie" blogs. Masculine or "manly" blogs focus on subjects such as politics, the military and war, and punditry. While men and women certainly cross over in their postings regarding these concerns, when it comes to blogging, there may indeed be a gender difference.

What educators and others know from decades of feminist research is that literacy continually rewrites the dominant cultural values regarding men and women. Whether reading and writing practices reinforce or alter gender stereotypes, shape passive or active learning behaviors in boys and girls, or shift the public-private dynamic in reading and composing texts can be debated. But what educators and scholars are clear on is that gender does affect the language and images used to communicate our attitudes, ideas, and beliefs. When these languages and images contradict cultural expectations for specific behaviors, we can either cling to tradition or transform the past.

Blogging is one area where literacy is rewriting cultural values and gender identification. No one ever knows for sure whether a blogger is male or female or whether the writer is defying gender expectations for effect. A myriad of personal, political, social, and cultural influences shape the decision of adopting a new persona; the body-less aspects of blogs just make the choice easier.

The decision to write in a feminine, masculine, or cross-gendered style is a conscious one. When writers actively select a particular gendered manner, they are attempting to move beyond an insular or local approach to the topic. Such decisions reflect a critical awareness of discourse-based literacies, as these choices carry certain consequences if an audience discovers that the writer is of a different gender than expected. Sometimes a blog site is subjected to vandalism, trolling, flaming, or bloggerel. (*Trolling* means leaving messages goading a writer and *flaming* means leaving hostile remarks. *Bloggerel* refers to crudely written posts designed to drive away visitors.)

Blog writing requires writers to examine their political stances, social roles, and cultural identities through the subjects they discuss. This inquiry can often extend into opening up one's gendered positions to the writing or thinking process. Sometimes bloggers' explorations reinforce cultural or gender stereotypes, but often these online conversations challenge the assumptions found in society. This is especially true when bloggers take on social roles different from the ones they maintain in real life. When bloggers adopt new online identities, particularly when young bloggers assume different personas drastically different than their actual personalities, educators and parents must ask themselves what perspectives are coming to light and why. Teachers and family members have to consider whose value system is present on a youngster's blog—that of the school, popular culture, the dominant society, or the family unit—and whose value system is silenced.

What recent studies have shown is that there are certain characteristic differences between blog sites self-identified as being written by females and those written by males. Whether these styles begin at adolescence and continue into adulthood will be addressed later in this chapter. For now, though, it is important to identify the rhetorical and linguistic features that mark a blog style as being "female" or "male."

THE FEMALE BLOGGING STYLE

Beyond centering on life or "kitchen table" concerns, the following are considered markers of a "female style" in blogging:

- A personal or confessional tone in opinion writing
- Frequent use of the first person (I) in writing
- Contextualization in terms of one's own life or experiences
- Individualized or "little" blog that becomes cross-linked with other similarly themed blogs
- Discussions as a means for bonding, sharing experiences, creating a community, or building empathy

The female blogging style parallels how linguists and discourse analysts describe female conversational style. Subjects are grounded in personal experience and often display an attempt to generate what linguist Deborah Tannen (1990) describes as "rapport talk."

THE MALE BLOGGING STYLE

If conversational styles correlate to blogging styles, then a "male style" for blogging should have features that parallel masculine discursive practices. The following features have been identified through a close study of blogs written by men:

- An agent-less, impersonal tone (use of the third person focused on the subject)
- Assumption that one's opinions are universally shared
- An unwavering or unyielding tone
- The use of *fisking* (This refers to the ruthless point-by-point refutation or criticism that highlights another writer's or blogger's errors.

When done well, fisking is witty, somewhat sarcastic, and logical.
When done poorly, fisking is snide and cynical in tone.)
- Contextualization in terms of current events, politics, foreign policy, war, and media issues
- An aggressive communication style filled with rough-and-tumble exchanges, some vulgarity or profanity, or crude jokes and references

The type of verbal play described here parallels the discursive strategies often connected to masculine language use. Masculine blogs attempt to talk in terms of power relations rather than in terms of a shared community. Tannen describes this phenomenon as "report talk," which centers on discussing or interrogating fact-based material.

While age and blogging experience seem to be a mediating factor in the blogger's overall style, one has to wonder whether these blogging styles are apparent at adolescence or whether they are acquired later, if at all. A recent thesis study conducted by Georgetown University's David Huffaker (2004) suggests that teenage blogging styles might not be as gender diverse as their adult counterparts. If Huffaker's research holds true, then blogging could transcend stereotypical gendering in language.

GENDER SIMILARITIES IN TEENAGE BLOGS

Huffaker proposes that there are important gender similarities between teenage boys and girls when they're blogging. In the just over 900 million current blogs, 52 percent are developed and maintained by 13- to 19-year-olds. And of that 52 percent, the gender split is basically even. So both teenage males and females maintain approximately 225 million blogs each.

With the volume of teenagers who are blogging, one would expect a high number of gender differences. However, Huffaker's dissertation research indicates that there are significant gender similarities among teenage bloggers. The sharing of personal data, contact information, and content is consistent. Another surprising gender similarity from Huffaker's study is that most active teenagers' blogs show a high level of loyal readers, in terms of visible posts and the length of posts (an average of 2,000 words per page). This is true whether the blogs are created by males or females. In fact, Huffaker found that boys' blogs were longer than those of their female peers. The word count for teen boys' blogs was 2,383.68, compared to 2,139.00 average words in teen girls' blogs.

Not only were the adolescent males' blogs more loquacious, they were also more inclined to use a wider vocabulary. Huffaker found that male blogs averaged 763.6 different words, compared with 666.2 different words found on females' blogs. The boys were also considered to be more flirtatious in their postings. But the content found on teenage boys' blogs was similar to the content found on teenage girls' blogs: school, relationships (boyfriends and girlfriends, crushes, intimate talk), sexual identity, and musical tastes.

Huffaker's findings are remarkable given Thomas Newkirk's 2002 study of boys' literacy. Newkirk explains that boys consider reading and writing not to be an engagement with the world but a retreat from the world. A similar result emerged from Michael W. Smith and Jeffrey Wilhelm's 2002 protocol study of boys and literacy. In those studies, boys who showed an interest in writing and reading thought it undermined their identities as "real boys." These researchers posited that boys wrote and read when it served a direct purpose, such as fixing a car or figuring sports statistics, or if it was connected to popular culture.

It may be that blogs are a form of writing and literacy that connects to teenage boys' interests. Various studies conducted over the past decade indicate that boys spend slightly more time on computers than girls, although this figure is shrinking. Because blog postings are short, frequent, and connect to an individual's interests, educators might discover that they can encourage reticent teenage male writers to compose. Teenage boys might view blogs as an acceptable mode of communication. They might see blog writing as a "fortunate opportunity to release a myriad of emotions in a zone of safety," as Harvard Medical School clinical psychologist William Pollack explains in his book *Real Boys' Voices* (2000, p. 369). Talking about sports, music, cars, or other "male" interests in a blogging environment might provide some boys with a sense that they are not alone in experiencing certain feelings or facing problems.

Decades of research have found that teenage boys maintain an absorbed or intensive relationship with their computers. Such absorption or intensity seems to extend to teenage boys' intrinsic online communication style in that boys consider blogs an arena for action and interaction between their cyber lives and real lives. Instead of viewing blogs as an instrument or tool for functional communication, teenage boys see them as a mode for discussing a range of different activities related to their lives, including schooling, socializing, and thinking. On blogs, boys can manage the flow of conversations and topics and therefore direct the space and time invested in talking about some issues compared to others. Therefore, it might be that boys also view blog postings as friendly messages that show how they relate to the world at large and how they control their lives on a daily basis.

GENDER DIFFERENCES IN TEENAGE BLOGS

Of course, gender distinctions arise in blogging, even in the teenage years. According to David Huffaker's research, the following are the most common linguistic difference between teenage male and female blogs:

- More males use emoticons to express emotions.
- More male than female teens "come out" sexually on blogs.
- More male than female teens give their geographic location on blogs.
- Males use more purposeful or definite language on their blogs.
- Males choose fantasy/mythical, sports-related, conceptual, or non-sensical nicknames as pseudonyms.
- Females select musical or popular culture nicknames or use their first names or a variation of their first names.
- When selecting an avatar (image or icon representing the blogger's identity), males choose an abstract image or graphic. Females select a realistic photo or graphic of a person. More than half of the male blogs examined in Huffaker's study had avatars; a bit less than half of the female blogs maintained an avatar.
- Male blogs more regularly reflect aggression, accomplishment, or

motion/activity. Female blogs encourage communicative responses or action.

The gender differences in blogs suggest there are differences between teenage boys and girls in the underlying social relationships and purposes for creating and maintaining the blogs. While both groups share personal information, particularly name, contact information, and school name, certain intimate data like sexual orientation or emotional state can reflect teenage boys' ability to use technology to amplify their feelings and ideas in an abstract format.

If research from the 1990s still holds, and I believe it does, teenage girls prefer telephone communication over computer communication for intimate conversations. Thus, cell phones and texting are preferred technologies for teenage girls' intimate discussions, as these modes are less abstract and allow for expression at a one-on-one level. Blogs, because of their relative anonymity, are a way for girls to transmit purposive or functional information, such as musical tastes, interest in popular movies or actors, and so on. Or, as I point out in the next chapter, blogs can become an instrument for spreading rumor and innuendo about classmates and rivals.

For teenage girls, the telephone might be a preferred mode of communication because of its spontaneity, mobility, and wider applicability compared to blogs. Gender research over the past decade has shown that women perceive the telephone as a medium that builds community and social networks. For young women, the telephone seems to be a preferred method for lending support, empathy, and counseling and maintaining relationships.

From a technological perspective, the telephone might be a teenaged girl's preferred communication method because of its almost universal access. Most homes have a phone, and with pay-as-you-go wireless and family cellular phone plans, teenage ownership of a cell phone is commonplace. With phones, teen girls don't have to spend hours learning a new technology to communicate, as some must to blog. Moreover, telephony reflects a young girl's developing sense of public versus private self. Cell phones and instant messaging rely completely on the user's control of who receives the messages, and as a result teenage girls better control their conversations. Even though adolescents often use their cell phones in public venues, girls see their conversations as private, especially when compared to the public disclosure of blogs in cyberspace. For that reason, it might be that for young girls, blogs present a public persona that can lead to more personal, off-blog conversations. As shown in Huffaker's study, blogs are a way for teenage girls to determine who will enter their inner circle of cell phone or IM buddies, technologies that render much more private and intimate discussions.

DOES AGE MATTER?

This chapter's focus on teenagers' blogs not only illustrates how middle or high schoolers use blogs to communicate, but it also gives teachers and parents a chance to see how their students and children grow into gendered communicative styles. Age matters because how teenage boys and girls use blogs often mirrors how adult men and women use other technologies to exchange information. Several research studies conducted over the last decade have found that asynchronous communication styles parallel face-to-face conversational styles, and that male and female discourse patterns are reflected in online environments.

Susan Herring's 1996 investigation of online communication styles uncovered that, as in real-time, real-life settings, the male discourse strategies of adversarial language, self-promotion, and a contentious or assertive tone also occur in asynchronous environments like blogs. Herring, like Huffaker, also discovered that male posts are longer and more frequent, with little concern for the rules that guide online discussions. Similar findings come from Cindy Selfe and Paul Meyer's 1991 study of academic listservs with regard to masculine conversational styles. Males who maintain high social status tend to dominate discussions. In adolescence, this may be a way for boys to practice conversational rituals that emphasize their status.

Correspondingly, these studies show that female conversational styles mirror real-time, real-life situations in asynchronous environments like blogs. Feminine discourse traits such as qualifying words or phrases and apologetic, supportive, or polite tones frequently appear in postings. The young women studied used the electronic writing space to build rapport and community rather than to engage in academic debate and verbal sparring.

Researchers have learned that peer socialization begun in childhood continues in the asynchronous communication space. This makes sense since blogs, like other electronic genres, are primarily social. Bloggers carry with them the socialization processes and conversational styles learned in prior social experiences. Therefore, teachers and parents who want their students or children to become effective online communicators need to pay attention to their charges' language and socialization patterns starting in childhood, since it appears that youngsters begin to learn about language and behavior well before they reach adolescence or blogging.

IMPLICATIONS FOR LITERACY BASED ON GENDER DIFFERENCES IN BLOGGING

From a literacy standpoint, the gender differences displayed by adolescents in their blogging behaviors suggest that a transformation is occurring. Blogs illustrate that teachers and parents can no longer define literacy only in terms of the academic or business world—what adults often refer to as the "real world." The linguistic strategies, subjects, and styles teenage bloggers use suggest that adolescents now structure their worlds on—quite literally—their own terms. Using the language of adolescents, bloggers address intense and honest assessments of the concerns and issues that surround teenage life. While administrators, teachers, and parents might not always like what they read on these students' blogs, these sites illustrate that the realities of teens' lives might not be the fond memories of high school and adolescence that many adults carry.

What is evident from reading blogs through a gendered lens is how carefully teenagers construct online personas to create a world they want to inhabit. Teachers and parents need to realize that these youngsters' "blog selves" might be very different from the child who sits in class or in front of the television each day. The blog becomes a place to begin negotiating the public and private identities on the way to becoming adults. On blogs, a shy child in the back of class might become an

online "playa"; similarly, the class clown could become a serious, reflec-
tive poet. The anonymity of blog space allows students to adopt new
identities without sacrificing the comfort of older ones. This might be
one reason why Huffaker found that a greater number of boys who blog
seem at ease in acknowledging their homosexuality: The protection of
an avatar or screen name permits them to test public reaction toward
their sexual coming-out.

Because school is a pivotal institution for most teenagers, teachers
and parents should not be surprised that students make it a focal topic
of discussion. Besides being an academic environment, school is the primary cultural and social space for most students. This is particularly so
in high school, where students first come into contact with various
power relations and dynamics, experience radical emotional shifts, and
occupy various subject positions. Students' perceptions of themselves
are affected by the words and deeds of peers more so than by the approval or disapproval of family members, as they were in the past.

Friendships in this context are frequently lively and fleeting, subject
to drama, questioning, and reflection. These characteristics make for
highly engaging stories or entries that relate to an adolescent audience.
While most school administrators, teachers, parents, and career bloggers find teenage blogs to be immature or maudlin (and indeed, compared to professional discourse, these blogs are syrupy, weepy, and
sometimes puerile), all of us must recognize that we judge these teenage voices from our own positions as adults. In order for blogs to influence student literacies, educators and parents need to understand that
the blogosphere must remain an arena where students can speak their
own language and have it valued before moving on to reconstructing
their experiences. Then, as students begin to question their positions
and beliefs, their blog content can change and adapt to mirror their own
growth.

Frequently in school settings, students find their own identities to be
transitory. One moment they are successful and the next they are struggling. On some days, they are complacent and on others they are resistant. By writing a blog, some students find the journaling process
helpful in sorting out these mixed feelings and messages. While many
students think their opinions rarely matter in school or in adults' eyes,
on a blog their views count for a great deal. Through feedback, whether
generated by in-class responses or through an external readership, com-

ments from blog readers can help young bloggers think through these situations. In these moments, students begin to write new or different chapters for their lives, which contributes to the growth educators and parents seek.

A student's preferred conversational style for blogging does not necessarily indicate that one gender has more or a better verbal facility than the other. It might suggest, however, that a student who prefers a less powerful conversational style might not find online environments like blogs to be a constructive place for learning. Teachers and parents should note that such a preference is not always grounded in biology.

Gender's digital divide has narrowed considerably, as most teenagers have grown up surrounded by computer technology. If a technological divide still exists in terms of gender, it might relate more to an individual's indifference to technology rather than to his or her access to a computer. This is a major reason why students have to be exposed to as many options for information and technology literacy as possible in their learning and writing experiences. Regardless of their gender, students have to determine which technology media and genres allow them to best articulate their attitudes, ideas, positions, and beliefs to a public audience.

Where gender differences appear to surface in relation to blogging is in the choice of interactive style—that is, whether the user sees a blog as a method for community building or for communication. Teenage girls who view blogs as a way to enhance their social networks, for instance, are more likely to create and maintain a blog. Teenage boys who build and maintain a blog usually do so because of the opportunity for "hands-on" learning through technology.

This significant gender difference regarding interactive style is an important aspect of classroom literacy. For educational environments that require students to blog, Huffaker's observation that males are more prolix than females is crucial. Earlier research from the United Kingdom (Kear & Heap, 1999) noted that courses where online communication is part of the curriculum showed that young women communicated less, contributed less frequently, did not receive the same levels of feedback, and did not seek out the same types of support mechanisms compared to their male peers. The data suggest that young girls may not always respond positively toward online communication in the classroom. Why this happens appears to be rooted in the teen girls' view that blogging and other electronic genres need to be grounded in building communities and social systems. Blogs function similarly to how adolescent girls view schooling—primarily as a social support system and network, not as an academic center.

Given that teenage girls value online communication mostly as a way to generate a social network and not as a learning tool, educators have to find ways to show adolescent females how blogs can shape communities in order for girls to value blogging. While boys often have an inherent motivator for blogging (its "hands-on" aspect), girls must be presented with a similar motivator. To reach girls, teacher and parents must present blogs as a flexible genre: a form that can perform both school and social functions.

Allowing teenage girls to construct blogs around popular cultural topics such as music, film, and fashion can provide them with incentives to write and to become more technologically literate. Teachers can encourage these girls to write critical or academic papers based on their exploration of popular culture.

Alternatively, collaborative or cooperative learning approaches to blogging can inspire young females to build and maintain blogs, since interacting with classmates often provides the social network needed to spark girls' interest in technology. These collaborative or cooperative strategies might include forming blog rings or using wikis, both of which depend upon mutual efforts among participants. A *blog ring* is a group of related blog sites linked together, so viewers who enter one blog can travel to other topic-related blogs. Sometimes there is a moderator who makes sure all the blogs are linked and related. A *wiki* is an interactive website that allows users to edit and change content in constructive collaborative writing (like the well-known Wikipedia). Wiki content changes every time users post new information, but the software allows users to revert information to a prior state if erroneous or harmful material is posted. Lore suggests that the term wiki comes from the Hawaiian term "very fast," so named after the transport buses at Honolulu airport. An alternative origin of wiki is an acronym for What *I* Know *Is*, a reference to the user's contribution to collective knowledge.

Building information or technology literacy means exploring further how genders engage in genres like blogging. Education researchers and

teachers still have much to learn regarding gender preference with certain electronic genres, such as IM, wikis, or blogs. Researchers and
teachers are just discovering how knowledge and information are transferred through these electronic genres and how the genders participate
and contribute to make shared meaning. As researchers, teachers, parents, and others venture further into the nexus between electronic communication and education, it will become increasingly more important
to outline specific kinds of learning in order to indicate student achievement in these new literacies. Certainly, as Huffaker's study suggests,
gender marks some communicative style and content issues. It also appears as though gender preferences exist for communication technologies. These areas can point educators toward learning more about
gender choices in the ways teenagers communicate.

Literacy runs throughout all human activity, regardless of historical
time or physical space, and from the days of cave dwellers scratching
images on stone with pieces of flint, technology has always been at the
center of literacy. The intersection of technology and literacy shapes
how writers and thinkers make meaning within a social system. Blogs
are merely the latest technological iteration. By themselves, blogs are
neither good nor bad, and neither are they ingenious nor trivial.

What makes blogs original is how they allow writers to create imagi-
native new worlds, identities, and knowledge. Such originality comes
not necessarily from the technology but from the ingenuity of the person using the form. Whether teenagers want to dominate a conversation
or build consensus, they can adapt a blog to their end goal—
communication.

In the classroom, a blog's worth comes from the ways teachers can
use this genre and technology to enhance their students' creative
thought processes and encourage all students, regardless of gender, to
develop important technological abilities. As blogs adapt to other electronic writing genres, educators and parents will continue to examine
how students use these media. Will gender be a factor of how creativity,
ingenuity, and originality in writing is expressed? Given that for most of
the last century gender has been part of literacy research, it seems
highly likely that future literacy studies will continue to explore the influence of gender on writing grounded in new technological literacies.

Any shift in literacy must be accompanied by some discussion of accountability regarding the use of blogs in the classroom and their connection to writing. While it is easy to measure surface growth through standardized writing tests, different and perhaps novel ways of thinking and learning are resistant to standardization. In fact, most educators, particularly those in higher education, know that standardized tests frequently punish innovative or creative thinkers because their ideas push beyond the expected or trite response. Will gender influence this area? Right now, it is too soon to say.

As more K–12 schools include information literacy in the curriculum, student achievement might have to be defined differently for teaching with blogs or wikis, as the significance of collaborative or cooperative learning experiences will increase, as will the students' higher-order thinking skills. Again, keeping track of gender similarities and differences can be an important part of determining what successful learning is. Providing a range of support options for future writing assessments in collaborative, electronic learning environments and emphasizing students' self-assessment can lead teachers, professors, and parents toward a better understanding of how gender influences traditional, information, and technological literacies for teenage boys and girls.

5

ETHNICITY AND BLOGGING

In most of the academic and popular literature on blogs, blogging is frequently thought to be a generational rather than a racial or ethnic activity. However, the statistics on tweens and teens who blog suggest a different conclusion. A 2004 Pew Internet study of teens (Rainie, 2004) as content creators and consumers reported that urban youth were the largest block of producers of shared Internet content (40 percent). The majority of this population was made up of girls between the ages of fifteen and seventeen from families with incomes under $30,000. Most of these girls kept blogs as an outlet for self-expression.

In the teen blogosphere, digital divides are closing. A 2005 Pew Internet study of teens (Lenhart & Madden) indicated that 17 percent of African American teens and 17 percent of Latino/a teens blog, compared with 19 percent of Caucasian teenagers. The study of teens and their technology use showed that Latino/a and Asian students tended to be online daily (89 percent of these teens surveyed, respectively) compared to African American students (77 percent).

A significant number of these students used computer access points at school or a public library if there was no computer connection in their homes. Therefore, the argument that urban teens who are minorities do not have a technological gateway seems dated given the findings from the 2004 and 2005 Pew Internet studies. Regardless of race or ethnicity, current-day adolescents are the most technologically connected ever. And if the statistics from these studies are correct, today's teenagers find ways to access the Internet even if their families have incomes that are on the lower end of the economic scale.

While teachers and parents may be isolated from the blogosphere (the 2005 Pew Internet study reports that nationwide, only 66 percent of adults venture online), urban minority students are not. Urban ethnic students are nearly as wired to society as their suburban White peers. The 2005 Pew Internet study on teens and technology use found that 84 percent of all adolescents have at least one media device (e.g., computer, cell phone, or personal digital assistant) that allows Internet access. Students are using these tools to blog, as well as to send instant messages or e-mail.

The findings from the Pew Internet studies suggest that any discussion of blogging and teaching writing would be incomplete without an examination of how ethnicity shapes teens' blog content and use. The connections between ethnicity and information and technological literacy are crucial ones to explore, especially if educators and parents hope to learn more about the linguistic and social practices of minority youth.

THE "HIPNESS FACTOR"

Blogging appeals to urban minority youth because of what I call a blog's "hipness factor"—an intangible quality that attracts widespread interest. The hipness factor is described as an elevated status where others wait impatiently to read, link, or connect to the daily or weekly postings found on someone's blog.

As with most cultural phenomena, if one has to ask whether blogs are hip or why a particular blog is hip, it's a guarantee that either the questioner or the blog certainly doesn't come close to being hip. From examining a number of teenagers' blogs, however, I have observed that the following factors typically determine whether a youngster's blog will have "the hipness factor":

- The blogger has his or her hand on the pulse of teenage life.
- The blogger displays a distinctive communicative style or personality.
- The blogger demonstrates great technological skill and facility on his or her site through high-quality graphics, sound, writing, and links related to the topic.

Colin Lankshear and Michele Knobel (2003) observed that competent bloggers are in step with the mood of the times. This quality certainly demonstrates whether a blogger is cool or not and enhances the perception of blogs as hip. The more in tune a blogger is with the pulse of a particular community or subculture, the more cool and therefore hip the blogger is.

Capturing the flavor of a moment depends in part on a blogger's ability to demonstrate an awareness—usually an ironic, wry, or parodic kind—of the events that surround the blogger. Blog postings are usually witty, snarky (i.e., humorous, but frequently irritable or mean in tone), and sometimes cynical. Like rap songs, poetry slamming, graffiti, or other verbal play that appeal to many urban youth, the hipness factor connects to being *cool*; that is, what is considered cool on blogs often relates to what Alan Liu (2004) describes as the "ego of information." The best way to explain Liu's phrase is, the grander the information and the more personality or sense of self on display, the better.

For minority adolescents, the hipness factor comes from adopting a cool pose, an attitude toward communicating stories (for example, how a young black woman in Newark, New Jersey, a tween Latino in East Los Angeles, or a teenage Native American on the reservation lives with and manipulates technology and information in a neighborhood). In this cool pose, the blogger's personality drives alternative presentations of the self and of the knowledge related to the community in which the teenager lives. Often minority teens' blogs are political, reflecting issues in the home or street community that may not be discussed during the school day.

In the teen blogosphere, coolness or hipness doesn't necessarily mean braggadocio. The hipness factor in blogging is not the same as what is considered hip in commercialized rap or hip hop music, which often encourages youngsters to make overblown, empty boasts. Being cool or hip in the teen blogosphere relates to one's skills or abilities rather than swagger or strut. The more a blogger demonstrates mastery of both controlling the information in his or her community and mastery over technology, the cooler or hipper the blogger. Mastery of technology is second only to mastery over cash. Cool or hip bloggers have "mad skillz"—a high or expert level of proficiency. While a number of minority students might not have mastery over cash flow, they can indeed develop the technological mastery necessary to be considered cool in the blogosphere.

Educators and parents might liken being cool in the blogosphere to feeling extremely comfortable in assembling, sharing, and delivering volumes of communal information. These students are information or knowledge producers—the ones who are "in the know." While such students may not be the most popular at school, in the blogosphere their sites are the places to visit. In turn, their online personas may be larger than life. Their identities are frequently tied to being "someone" in the teenage blogosphere.

Students who attain such coolness through their blogs acquire the hipness factor they so often seek in real life. A blog that has the hipness factor surpasses being cool; it becomes high status, which brings the blogger much recognition because of his or her sense of style, facility with technology, and connection to the times. The hip student blogger is more than cool; he or she taps into the hearts, minds, and attitudes of other students, expresses their opinions or interests, tells their stories, and arouses their curiosities.

BRIDGING VERNACULAR AND SCHOOL CULTURES

For many minority teenagers, blogs offer the social, spiritual, and intellectual outlets that they cannot find during the school day. Rather than risk alienating middle-class Caucasian teachers or classmates by expressing different viewpoints, these teenagers can use a blog as a place to right the wrongs they face on a daily basis.

Educators and parents can encourage minority students to think of blogging as an opening or passage to discuss larger social justice issues in their lives. It is not too difficult a task for teachers or parents to design effective writing prompts for students. A useful writing prompt allows the writer to enter a discussion from a particular point of view or set of experiences. The difficulties that large numbers of minority students have with standardized writing prompts are that the situations or contexts rarely connect with their lives. Blogging becomes an excellent replacement for abstract prompts because the students can write from their lives and broaden the experiences to reach out to other readers. A teacher who provides directed blogging tasks should consider having students address topics more applicable to their lives.

Asking students to write about topics more pertinent to their lives does not mean having students drift into banalities. On the contrary, students who write about subjects more germane to their experiences may write more evocatively and thoughtfully, depending on the prompt. Writing from their experiences, students can express their views on a range of topics, such as the differences between racial self-hate and group-based racial hatred; why violence and rage are often the answers to social problems in certain communities; or why the language of soul describes both love and anger. In addition, on blogs, minority teens have the opportunity to write about self-esteem issues that they often face: the range of beauty in women and men of color; the histories and ideologies of Black, Latino/a, Native American, or Asian cultural figures; and the stories of ordinary people.

Blogging in this manner provides a means for a significant number of students to write passionately and reflectively on topics that bridge home and school cultures. While many of these students cannot relate to William Golding's *Lord of the Flies* or John Knowles' *A Separate Peace*, the usual high school literary fare that determines students' academic success, they can present long and thoughtful commentaries on the artistry of Tupac, Miles Davis, Langston Hughes, or Nikki Giovanni; the politics of Che Guevara, Hiram Rhodes Revels, or Aung San Suu Kyi; or the scientific contributions of George Washington Carver, Benjamin Banneker, or Karen Medville. They can speak with eloquence about the plight of Leonard Pelletier, the courage of those living on the Rez, or of Wounded Knee. By examining the successes of these important figures, minority students can discover their heritage and use this knowledge to bridge the worlds of school and home.

Moreover, for financially strapped school districts, harried teachers, and concerned parents, blogs serve as an inexpensive instrument to build the writing fluency and skills of traditionally underachieving student populations. Because blogging begins with writing short bursts of text that usually lead to additional entries, weaker writers can enter into the experience with some confidence. As their blogging skill increases, these writers can then be encouraged to post longer and more complex entries.

For those teachers who follow writing methodologies, the built-in publishing feature of blog software makes the writing experience meaningful for minority students, many of whom are apathetic about academic writing because they feel that the class work that they do is not relevant to their lives. If educators and parents want all students to develop a commitment toward writing, then it becomes crucial to develop a system that encourages all students to see how the written word can help them make their way in the world. Texts that can be produced by students, like blogs, provide the basis for cultivating a writing-reading environment that is meaningful and valuable for those students when traditional school literature seems too abstract, distant, or improbable compared to the lives they lead.

Once students become invested in blogging, educators and parents can incorporate vernacular writing into the school curricula. At this stage, students have become intellectually engaged in directed blogging tasks, and teachers and parents are starting to understand the youngsters' perspectives after reading the blogs. As a result, the process of helping students build a relationship with more traditional, academic texts is made easier. Stories, whether told by the literary masters or by teenagers whose lives are affected by violence, distrust, abuse, or other societal ills, offer readers insight into the human condition. Blogging gets students to the "human" or "real" aspect of writing and prepares them for reading seemingly more distant school literature.

When literary works are set in the context of everyday life or in terms of how the larger stories reflect daily life, all students—but particularly minority students—develop a better understanding of the material. Teachers can compare the emotional connections between blogging and reading to the emotional connections readers have with literary texts. These linkages are important for students to discover the power of the written word in all its forms, whether print or electronic.

ASKING AT-RISK STUDENTS TO TAKE RISKS IN THEIR WRITING

Regardless of what measures teachers, administrators, and parents use, educational statistics show that minority youth are in the at-risk category for learning. Many urban minority male and female students are placed in alternative education settings, such as special education classes. Achievement scores on the last two documented National Association of Educational Progress (NAEP) tests show across-the-board gaps when the progress of Caucasians is compared with that of Native American, African American, and Latino/a students (National Center for Educational Statistics, 2004). In several states across America, minority students' statewide assessment scores on language arts tests show underperformance. Lastly, fewer numbers of minority teenagers are going on to college after graduation, because of financial or academic concerns.

An entire generation of students from specific segments of the nation's population is not receiving the instruction needed to attain proficiency in writing. This does not have to happen, nor should this happen. Teachers and parents can push for change in raising minority students' writing scores, and promoting blogging technology for these youths can be a place to start.

One reason why these scores are repeatedly low can be traced to the use of outdated or culturally biased writing prompts. Students who have no knowledge of certain topics—such as basements in homes, the custom of brushing one's long, silky hair with one hundred strokes, or snow days in the South—struggle to write about things with which they have never come into contact. If the standardized writing prompts asked students to write a letter to the mayor regarding cleaning up a city's crack den so children could play basketball or double Dutch in the evening, the scores might be different.

The risks students take when they write about unfamiliar topics frequently result in lower scores, as most writing specialists will explain that students who do not have a grasp of the topic often cannot carefully articulate a position. In short, student writers cannot write well about those things they do not know. While the chances are slim that students will ever write a letter to a city mayor asking the council to clean up drug-ridden streets so children can play safely, urban students can use blogs to write about such topics to learn how to express themselves clearly and articulately in writing.

At-risk students can write well if they are introduced to a writing genre that gives students access to genuine, relevant experiences. All too frequently, these students do not see the value writing has in their lives. School writing is too abstract or distant from these students' lives. This is a second reason why minority students frequently underperform on state writing assessment tests.

Blogging can offer a starting point for showing students that writing can have a real purpose and readership. Because blogging connects students to real audiences, blogging may be an effective method of learning for at-risk students who need to improve their writing skills. While it may be true that blog postings will be written in vernacular language, teachers and parents have to realize that this mode of communication is a starting point, not an ending point for encouraging at-risk students to write. First, students have to begin communicating with the languages they have at their disposal. Once students display both mastery of the technology and the writing process, then educators and parents can move students forward in developing posts using standard American English.

A third reason why large numbers of at-risk students perform poorly on standardized writing tests stems from cultural and personal interference. Family, neighborhood, and individual problems frequently intrude in these students' lives. At-risk students often do not have effective mechanisms for handling their emotional reactions to serious life situations, such as early deaths because of street or domestic violence; adolescent pregnancy; parental divorce, alcoholism, abuse, or drug use; drastic shifts in the family's economic health or stability; family or personal health crises; and so forth. Add to these issues more typical adolescent concerns such as self-esteem, peer pressure, and school factors, and it is not too difficult to see that some at-risk students must overcome incredible odds to succeed in school.

Because blogging allows students to explore expressive writing— writing from emotions or experiences—a blog can become a therapeutic outlet for many at-risk students. Students who blog from an expressive standpoint discover that blogging becomes a positive way to handle the emotional pain that interferes with their learning. For some adolescents, writing an expressivist-based blog emerges as a method for clarifying their thoughts, discovering insights into their confusing worlds, and finding a voice when they feel silenced in other parts of their lives.

Whether the students write daily diary entries, poetry, or fiction, the idea of using a blog to release the emotions that constrict some at-risk students is the same. By offering these students an opportunity to release some of the conflict and tension they have inside, educators and parents provide a constructive mechanism for at-risk students to reduce their ongoing stress. For some students, this type of writing helps them refocus on schoolwork; for other students, expressivist writing becomes the start for directing them toward more academic writing. The goal for having emotionally at-risk students blog is to encourage them to think about writing in this manner: "When I write, I think about. . . ." Once students can articulate those points, teachers, parents, or other support staff can move students toward success rather than failure.

Throughout this chapter, I have argued that teachers should use blog assignments to encourage urban youth to write regularly and fluently. The notion that teachers and parents can use the vernacular culture found on most blogs as a bridge to writing on more academic subjects is not new; successful high school and college programs have been working with students to write critically from popular cultural sources since the 1970s. This time, however, students are being asked to demonstrate writing and technological proficiency. Such requests are not intended to be gimmicky; rather, for most states, technological facility is a clearly stated part of the core curriculum content standards all K–12 schools must meet.

Beyond encouraging real audiences who can provide responses or giving students productive outlets to write about their emotions, why else do blogs offer at-risk students hope for building writing skills? Let me offer five reasons, all of which I will expand upon in the remainder of this chapter:

- Students can work at their own pace.
- Students who are not successful in the rigid social atmosphere of a classroom can perform under a different structure, such as informal learning.
- Students who may not interact well with peers can find other audiences with whom they can engage in discussion and build the social networks they need and want as writers.
- Students can become lifelong learners and knowledge producers, learning anytime and anywhere.
- Students pay attention to their language use, grammar, and mechanics when they know a real audience is reading.

The first reason, students can work at their own pace, is crucial for engaging at-risk students. Students from minority or educationally disadvantaged backgrounds who find themselves labeled "at-risk" need to have a different schedule compared to more academically prepared or supported students. This does not mean educators and parents should have lower expectations for academically at-risk students; rather, writing assignments need to be more flexible and individualized. Quite frequently, at-risk students display different intelligences, interests, and strengths compared to more traditional or mainstream students. Usually, at-risk students are less structured in their approaches to learning content and some might be more autodidactic than their peers.

Blogging, then, can help these students pace their learning. Students have the opportunity to design and redesign a blog template to fit their learning or visual needs. In addition, the freedom to search out and write on academic subjects the students find interesting or appealing allows them to explore new avenues—something very important for autodidactic or highly creative students, many of whom are labeled at-risk because they do not conform well to the traditional quiescent student role.

As these students learn material, they can write reflectively and authoritatively on what they discover. They can ponder and revise their thinking as they acquire knowledge, which for some at-risk learners is important. Such a process encourages both active thinking and critical thinking, two activities that are often forsaken during the traditional class schedule because of tight adherence to curriculum standards. Autodidacts or highly creative students need time to think actively and critically; when that time is shortchanged because of curricular pressures, they lash out or become reticent students.

Of course, not all at-risk students are autodidactic or highly creative. Some are disorganized and unfocused in their approach to learning. For those students who tend to jump from topic to topic, a blog can be adapted to that learning style as well. These students usually have quick minds and can make associations among large volumes of text. They are highly active learners, but do not necessarily have attention deficit disorder. Rather, these students are incredibly efficient at processing information and thrive on the stimulation of learning new things. The more information they can process, the better.

Teachers and parents of lightning fast thinkers realize how quickly these students grow bored with traditional classroom learning experiences. Blogging allows these students the flexibility to move across subject areas at a rate that corresponds to their changing interests. As a result, these students tend to spend more time learning and they enjoy this informal approach far more than structured study.

In either instance, blogging promotes a learning environment where at-risk students have the opportunity to ask more questions, take greater ownership of their learning experiences, and move through information in a nonembarrassing or nonthreatening manner. For students who are labeled at-risk because of their strong autodidactic or creative needs, blogging is important because it permits students to learn through their choices of what to study. This is also true for the disorganized but quick learner. The writing, then, emerges as a chronicle of their minds at work or at play as these students present their work openly to the world. In the blogging process, these students not only teach themselves, they teach others as well.

Some at-risk teenagers, particularly strong autodidacts and creative types, bristle at the highly structured school day. Their resistance goes beyond the simple refusal to do homework. Many skip school altogether in search of other activities that connect to their interests. These students learn by doing, by engaging in hands-on tasks. Traditional schooling rarely has the type of tactile or concrete application of information some students crave. Typical classroom learning usually focuses on the abstract or theoretical, the distanced or nuanced idea rather than direct involvement.

Blogging addresses this need that resistant at-risk students have. To create a blog, students must be personally involved in the design and application of the software or templates. Learning to blog and maintaining a blog are hands-on processes. There is a high level of tactile stimulation with keyboarding; and at the end of a blogging session, there is tangible evidence of effort. For autodidacts or artistic types, blogging can be a way to learn and to create original material.

In contrast to the traditional school approach, such learning is considered informal, and it compares to the type of learning most individuals have on the job. With blogging, there is a demonstrated productivity level that appeals to students who like to learn in informal settings. Students can set a particular goal for their blogs, and they can construct a learning space through blogging that is both communal and expresses their competencies. Informal learning often appeals to at-risk students because it feels relevant to the students' goals and interests. Moreover, the informal learning environment dramatically changes the student-teacher relationship.

Rather than viewing blogging as a means for replicating the traditional classroom, teachers who blog with at-risk students need to see blogging as a type of instructional conversation, one in which participants build a learning community that includes both home and school contexts. In instructional conversation, teachers have to think that students can do more than just simply regurgitate facts or engage in stereotypical "kid speak." Teachers have to listen carefully to the students, determine appropriate conversational responses, and discuss how students' home, cultural, and intellectual lives connect with the knowledge the student presents.

Consequently, if teachers adopt the instructional conversational model for blogging with their at-risk students, they must set aside the "assign and assess" model that dominates current U.S. pedagogical practice. That means teachers must put themselves at some risk in the blogging process as well, since they will have to share elements of their own home, cultural, and intellectual lives to converse with their students. While many teachers may be uncomfortable with such a classroom transformation, for those who are at ease in sharing parts of their personal lives with students, blogging can forge new classroom experiences.

The instructional conversational model in blogging may also be important for Caucasian teachers who work with minority students. The focus on building talk that explores students' ideas rather than supplants questions from teachers' test banks seems to promote high levels of interaction in culturally and linguistically diverse classrooms.

As some Africentric pedagogical studies have shown, minority students interpret the directions. According to Africentric theory, minority students frequently find the speech patterns of white instructors to be insensitive, disrespectful, ambiguous, and nonauthoritative. Through blogging, the potential exists for teachers to bridge the cultural divides that occur in the classroom by providing a rich textual environment where instructors and students can learn from one another.

Instructional conversation may also be a key component for helping students who have difficulty with creating social networks in school and thus need other audiences for their writing. Blogs can be a perfect genre for establishing an external readership and fostering that talk-write connection to help these students form pro-social networks.

Clearly, the reasons for encouraging minority and at-risk students to blog are varied. However, if teachers or parents were to summarize the four main reasons why these students should blog, the top contenders would be the following:

- Blogging makes learning and writing relevant for these students.
- Blogging helps students acquire crucial technological skills.
- Blogging allows students to learn at their own pace.
- Blogging helps students form positive self-identities and pro-social networks in schools.

Educators and parents need to encourage minority youth to enter the blogosphere, as blogging is an important pathway for developing the technological and communication skills needed to succeed in higher education and in the workplace. Anthony Walton (1999) makes a cogent observation regarding the place of minority teens in cyberspace:

> If blacks are to survive as full participants in this society, they have to understand *and apply* what works *now*. Otherwise they will be unable to cross the next technological threshold that emerges in human civilization. Blacks have to imagine ways to encourage young people into the techno-logical mainstream, because that looks like the future. In fact, it always has been the future, and blacks, playing catch-up yet again, must reach for it to ensure themselves a place at the American table.

While Walton clearly addresses the concerns of Black Americans, his point also extends to Native American, Latino/a, and Asian students as well as economically disadvantaged Caucasian students. Blogging matters for minority students not just because it makes them hip and cool, but because they are learning how to use the technology that works now and will be able to transition to using future technology. Moreover, as these students focus on the future, they are learning and acquiring the writing, information, and communication skills that will make them successful in the present and in the years ahead.

6

BLOGS AND BULLYING

In the old days, bullies used to roam schoolyards during lunch, recess, and after class trying to pick fights or steal items. Most of us remember one or two individuals who displayed brutal or cruel behaviors toward particular classmates. Usually the instigators were insecure boys who were out to prove that they were tougher, meaner, and stronger than a physically weaker or socially isolated child. Or, in some instances, the bullies were mean-spirited girls who gossiped, sniped at, taunted, or played tricks on those they saw as social outcasts.

In the past, dads and moms believed that the only way to handle a bully problem was to take control of the situation. Parents used to tell their children to stand up for themselves when harassed and stop being a target—whether that meant walking away or hitting the bully first. That advice sometimes worked. When it didn't, an adult stepped in quickly and settled the score.

Today, though, educators and parents know a little more about why children bully. In the past decade, psychologists and educators discovered that most schoolyard bullies are or have been abused children, and they use aggression and hostility to lash out against the violence or rejection that they face at home. Still, not every child who bullies comes from a "bad environment." Some preteens and teenagers who intimidate or bother others come from solid homes. Why these children decide to inflict physical or emotional harm on their classmates is subject to debate. When these preteens and teens are smart and able to use technology to bully, the problem is widespread and can have long-lasting effects.

Between 65 and 90 percent of children aged nine to fourteen have had some experience with online bullying at some point, either as a victim or a perpetrator (Smith, 2005). Virtually all preteens and teens know of at least one student who has been involved in a cyberbullying incident. Certainly these figures suggest that cyberbullying is a pervasive student concern in schools, even though research studies indicate that only between 15 and 20 percent of adults (teachers, administrators, and parents) know cyberbullying exists (Aftab, 1999; Smith, 2005). Adults' general lack of knowledge about bullying in the new millennium contributes to much of this problem in schools.

THE NEW BULLY IN THE SCHOOLYARD

Stereotypes abound regarding the bully. The usual depiction of a bully is generally a male, perhaps a struggling student, who has poor relationships with his teachers and fellow classmates. Cyberbullies don't necessarily fit this description, however. Many times, children who bully others through online means are shy, nonconfrontational students in the classroom. With great regularity, cyberbullies are girls and honor students—two school subcultures that defy the typecast image of a bully.

The mainstream media often describe cyberbullying as "the revenge of the nerds," a takeoff on the title of a 1980s movie that demonstrated how school misfits get even with their more socially adjusted peers. The problem with such characterizations is that these descriptions marginalize the concerns students have about maintaining a sense of peace and self-respect when they are attacked in the blogosphere.

These old generalizations and clever cultural references about bullying and bullies contribute to how adults—that is, administrators, teachers, and parents—define intimidation in school. As long as there is no physical interaction, many adults do not consider the actions of a bully to be threatening. After all, if fists aren't being traded, then the only things thrown are words. And, as the ancient rhyme goes, "sticks and stones may break my bones, but names can never hurt me." In the case of cyberbullying, though, the constant insults, derogatory images, and incessant harassment can not only hurt victims, it can lead them to a breaking point, causing harm to themselves as well as to others.

Too often, educators and parents think of the traditional bully as someone with low self-esteem. The dominant view is that a bully often winds up in serious legal or personal trouble if no intervention is sought. These days, however, a good number of bullies have gone high-tech. Many savvy school administrators and teachers are well aware that the stereotypical bully is not the only tormentor in a classroom. There is, quite literally, a new kid on the block who frightens, threatens, or terrorizes his or her peers. Cyberbullies, those who intimidate classmates through blogs, Instant Messenger, or e-mail, use available computer technologies to browbeat and harass their victims. With electronic tools like anonymizers, which permit someone to send anonymous e-mails, or false e-mail accounts that allow senders to cloak their identities on blogs or e-mail, cyberbullies can hit their victims hard and fast, usually leaving no trace of who is sending the scary, upsetting, or oppressive posts.

With the help of technology, it is very easy for a cyberbully to escape detection. As any preteen or teenager can attest to, cyberbullies are quite the opposite of the traditional bully: Cyberbullies are smart, "good" students. Frequently, they are honor roll students or those who are popular with their classmates. A cyberbully could also be the shy child who sits quietly in the front row of the class and does his or her work. And, unlike the schoolyard bullies of the past, cyberbullies are often highly successful, popular females.

These high-tech intimidators are able to use their personal, social, and academic strengths to avoid detection. In the meantime, they conduct regular, systematic attacks on their victims as a way to gain social control, revenge, or power over their classmates. Such bullying activity is more than an attempt to impose clique-like behavior upon unwilling students. Sometimes these cyber assaults cause the victims to transfer schools, withdraw from normal activities, drop out of school, or in the worst cases, commit suicide.

WHAT DOES A CYBERBULLY LOOK LIKE?

Cyberbullies, unfortunately, look and act like most other adolescents. In fact, in a classroom full of students, a teacher, administrator, or parent might be hard-pressed to select those students who are or have been guilty of cyber abuse. An adult cannot identify cyberbullies by their appearance. Most tweens and teens will attest to cyberbullies often being honor students—the students least thought of as the ones who would engage in any sort of bad behavior.

Still, research in the area shows an emerging picture of what type of preteen or teenager may engage in these emotionally abusive practices (Aftab, 1999; Smith, 2005). These findings may be shocking to those who are used to viewing bullies as tough.

A typical cyberbully is between nine and fourteen years old and can be either male or female. A number of research studies have found that cyberbullying starts in the late elementary or junior high school years and continues until the early part of high school. The middle school years seem to be the peak period for cyberbullying activities (Aftab, 1999; Smith, 2005).

Many times, preteens who obtain their first Instant Message account or blog site use cyberbullying to see how far they can go online—a type of "pushing the envelope" behavior—before they are reprimanded. In these instances, unintended cyberbullying happens as these novice users adopt different personas or try out new social roles in an online environment. A few may even see cyberbullying as a way to joke or tease their friends; however, if the recipient of a hostile or threatening message does not recognize the sender or realize that the post was sent in jest, then the situation can turn serious and cause harm.

Certainly there are some tweens and teens who send harassing or intimidating posts just because they can. These students' motives are quite different from those of an inadvertent cyberbully. Under the cloak of anonymous e-mail, false names, or avatars, these individuals repeatedly post insulting comments about the victim. Adolescents who use blogs or other Internet tools to harass and oppress their classmates cloak their actions in ways that traditional bullies cannot.

A large number of these posts border on the sociopathic in that the content is marked by extreme antisocial thoughts directed toward a particular youngster. It is not uncommon for victims to find messages telling them to die, to fear walking the school halls, or to expect violence or rape. While on the surface the messages may appear to be from different senders, often the intended target knows or has a strong suspicion of who is sending the material.

Some interpersonal relationship experts describe this type of behavior as "relational aggression," a form of conduct that can begin in the elementary grades. Usually, but not always, cyberbullying stops in the later high school years. According to Aftab (1999), if cyberbullying continues past age fourteen, it tends to be in the form of sexual harassment. In general, cyberbullies can be categorized in the following ways:

Vengeful angels tend to right the wrongs they find at school.

Mean girls are bored and use blogs or other Internet tools to create rumors or innuendo for entertainment. These girls tend to display relationally aggressive behaviors in their posts.

Power-hungry nerds are often successful male students who use their intelligence and technological know-how to get revenge on traditional bullies who pick on them. Like mean girls, power-hungry nerds inflict relational aggression on their victims.

Some cyberbullies, like those who see themselves as vengeful angels, attempt to defend those who are picked on in school. However, in their attempts to right these moral wrongs, they create a far worse situation. Unlike mean girls or power-hungry nerds, these cyberbullies are motivated by good intentions, but their "good" deeds can escalate quickly into a hellish nightmare for others.

Most cases of cyberbullying fall under the category of relational aggressive behaviors. Relational aggression is a form of emotional abuse where bullies adopt psychological tactics to manipulate, terrorize, or destroy their peers. Common relationally aggressive acts like gossiping, taunting, spreading lies and rumors, or deliberately making friends with a peer to exclude that person from social events happen each day in a number of school classrooms. Often peer, teacher, or administration intervention can stem the problems early on before significant psychological damage is done to a student. Offenders can be sent to counselors, peer mediators, or administrators who can handle behavioral problems within the school.

When these acts are committed through a blog or e-mail, however, a constant barrage of messages or posts fills a child's space with few ways for him or her to control the flow. Because much of cyberbullying happens out of school and after the school day, any watchful adult eyes may be elsewhere. Even if the parents are home or the child is in an after-school program in the school library, the computer may be located in an unsupervised area, and the youngster has free access to sending or receiving harmful posts. Those parents or educators who closely monitor children's online use should not be too smug, however. Common terms used for online teenage communication like POS (parent over shoulder) may not be understood or recognized by tech-savvy adults. In short, if a preteen or teenager wants to cyberbully, he or she will find a way.

Unchecked by adults, these messages wreak havoc on a youngster's psychological growth. For preteens and teens who are just beginning to develop a sense of self, malicious postings reinforce the humiliating feelings—a sense of disparagement or belittlement, or negative self-perceptions that most adolescents have from time to time. The cyberbully preys upon these emotions in an attempt to wield social power over others.

Generally, the cyberbully uses the anonymity of blogging or e-mail to disseminate information that could be considered harassment or verbal assault. Such secrecy allows "mean girls" to flourish. Girls who bully on-line tend to comment about another's physical appearance or leave derogatory messages on the victim's blog or website. These girls also write embarrassing e-mail messages or spread rumors about their targets. These posts are then sent to blogs, chat rooms, or electronic lists. Frequently the contrived e-mails or blog posts focus on insults about the victim's friends or the victim, crushes, or sexual activity. In "milder" cases of cyberbullying, girls exclude their victims from Instant Messenger lists or send instant messages using the victim's IM account.

Psychologists theorize that girls gravitate toward relational aggression because American culture does not sanction intense competition and conflict among young females. Because popular stereotypes about female behavior still exist, such as girls are supposed to be nice, friendly, and pleasant, relational aggression flourishes. Girls in the preteen and early teen years value high levels of popularity. Girls who see themselves as challenged by a rival believe that they must treat their adversary discreetly by using culturally appropriate ways to harm the competitor. Consequently, cyberbullying is an ideal method for inflicting abuse on an opponent.

Although relational aggression tends to be more dominant in adolescent girls, boys are also susceptible to this type of behavior. Rather than attacking with words, boys frequently draw upon images to bully. With personal technologies like camera phones and digital cameras, cyber-

bullies can take photos of unsuspecting teens and, with little to no effort, create images or avatars of imaginary bullies to torment their peers.
Using common software like Photoshop and the images taken with cell
phones or digital cameras, these aggressors often doctor photos that
show students in sexual or compromising situations. Or, equally frequently, these bullies will create online profiles of a victim and send
contact or other personal information to various websites.

A technologically proficient cyberbully can create a range of avatars
or personas to trash a victim. As a result, victims may never truly know
who is at the center of these attacks. The abuser could be a "best
friend," a close classmate, or someone who preys upon anyone who is
different, so victims have no idea how to protect themselves from the
next incident. Although some students may see such images as a joke,
others may not view the situation that way. Cognitive researchers at
Stanford University discovered that women and men process images
differently (BBC, 2005). Females recall images with more dramatic
clarity and process images in nine parts of the brain, while males process
images in two parts of their brains. Because of the differing cognitive
processes, these doctored images can stay with the victim for a long
period, particularly if the target is female.

Another type of male relational aggressor that exists online is known
as a "griefer." Such individuals taunt others or form online gangs to target or harass someone just for fun. A griefer frequently uses inappropriate language toward a victim or constructs various online annoyances to
irritate a user. Griefers often lurk on gaming sites where they hone in
on new players, but they can be in a classroom as well. Griefers can also
send general bodily threats, leave malicious posts on a victim's blog, or
start "warning wars" or "notify wars" on gaming sites. (A warning war
or notify war is a series of exchanges that begin when a griefer reports
a target for service violations at a game site. These wars escalate quickly
and often spread to other users, creating a type of collateral damage to
a number of victims.)

Unlike traditional forms of bullying where a child can see the attacker, cyberbullying is anonymous, cruel, and ruthless. Often cyberbullying breaches conventional social boundaries, a situation that
contributes to the target's emotional trauma. For example, rarely is
there any face-to-face contact between the tormentor and the victim.

This makes it difficult, if not impossible, for a victim to ignore, refute, or confront the abuser. Nearly all cyberbullying is psychological in nature, and these acts of torture are easy to refute. Besides an outright denial of cyberbullying, a cyberbully can say his or her online identity or passwords were stolen and used to create a persona that allowed a third party to intimidate a fellow student.

For victims who may already be ostracized by their peers, trying to challenge a cyberbully who denies culpability is one more socially isolating maneuver, especially if the adults who are in contact with the victims see emotional anguish as trivial or not as damaging as physical pain. Cyberbullies thrive in school environments where adults consider these verbal and visual assaults as simply teenage annoyances. Thus, students, educators, and parents must understand that the type of bullying that happens online is far more complicated and agonizing for victims than mere schoolyard taunts or pestering.

WHAT HAPPENS WHEN CYBERBULLYING GOES TOO FAR

Cyberbullying brings out a dark side of adolescents that adults either are unaware of or they choose to ignore. Educators and parents may discount a child's concerns about being attacked online because they see the problem as one that parallels the "sticks and stones" reference made earlier in this chapter. Other adults tend to overlook adolescent social problems, thinking that many of these issues are just part of growing up. Then there are those grown-ups who take no notice of youngsters' difficulties, either because they do not encounter preteens or teens on a regular basis or they have pressing concerns that dominate their lives.

For any number of reasons, it is incredibly easy for adults to close their eyes to cyberbullying until a crisis or a tragedy makes the news headlines. Then suddenly, adults take notice and comment on the sad state of teenagers' lives. What is sad, however, is not that these children's lives ended tragically or that a crisis took over a local school. The heartrending part is that any child was ever subjected to the type of emotional abuse inflicted by cyberbullies.

To illustrate the mental and emotional anguish as well as physical destruction that can happen from endless streams of abusive online content, accounts from three well-documented and publicized cases of cyberbullying are presented. While cyberbullying crosses both gender lines, the more highly noticed accounts involve teenage males. Perhaps it is the violent or disturbing conclusions to boys' cyberbullying that attract the most attention, or perhaps more people consider young girls more likely candidates for cyberstalking or online predators and so they focus on stories about these issues rather than on cyberbullying. Regardless of the victim's gender, the lives and crises of Ryan Halligan, Ghyslain Raza, and William Freund are instructive stories for educators and parents because they illustrate well the potentially devastating effects of cyberbullying on all teenagers.

For those adults who believe that the following three instances are isolated, sensationalized cases, let me state that similar events happen every day in schools throughout the United States and the world. Cyberbullying is a global problem, and the issue looms larger in schools each year as more students gain Internet access. The stories of Ryan Halligan, Ghyslain Raza, and William Freund are cautionary tales that are presented to inform adults and children about the collision course occurring between adolescents and cyberspace.

Cautionary Tale #1: Ryan Halligan

In 2003, a suicide caused by cyberbullying was one of the first to be nationally publicized. Ryan Halligan, a thirteen-year-old boy from Essex Junction, Vermont, hanged himself after months of cyber torment. According to published news reports in *Boston* magazine (Voss, 2006), the *Philadelphia Inquirer* (Pappas, 2005), and the *Las Vegas Review Journal* (Whiteley, 2005), the teenager was harassed and attacked physically in school because of a learning disability and a lack of bodily coordination.

Ryan's disabilities made him different from other students. It also seemed that his differences made him more subject to attack. However, he fought back when some of his male classmates started hallway altercations. Perhaps Ryan's unwillingness to be a victim led to what happened next.

When physical abuse didn't frighten him, the students turned to emotional cruelty. One of the boys befriended the teen and then used personal medical information that Ryan had shared with the boy to spread a rumor that Ryan was gay.

Other students at Ryan's school saw him as a target for abuse as well. A female classmate, reportedly a popular girl at school, pretended to like the teenager. She then disseminated all the private e-mails the boy sent to her, and the girl's circle of friends joined in the harassment. The e-mail and Internet attacks escalated from there and lasted throughout seventh grade and into eighth grade.

Halligan refused to take his problems to school administrators, fearing his problems would worsen. A teacher who saw students harassing the teen failed to step in because she saw no overt physical violence. Still, a problem clearly existed. Ryan's father acknowledged that toward the end of his son's life, the boy suffered from depression. Ryan had surfed websites that focused on suicide, and according to a report filed with the Canadian Internet news blog outlet, *Citizens Voice* (www .citizenvoices.gg.ca), Ryan sent posts to his peers that indicated he was prepared to commit suicide as a way to get back at his harassers. In a final Instant Message to his tormentors, Ryan purportedly typed, "Tonight's the night," a reference to his impending death. An Instant Message response from one of the cyber abusers said, "It's about time."

Cautionary Tale #2: Ghyslain Raza

In 2002, a widely downloaded short film on the Internet titled "The Star Wars Kid" circulated worldwide. In the clip, Ghyslain Raza, an overweight, bespectacled fifteen-year-old is shown wielding a golf club as if it were a Jedi light saber. Within months, more than fifteen million downloads of the two-minute-long video appeared on computer screens in schools, colleges, and offices everywhere.

The clip is still available on the Internet for viewing, and Ghyslain has gained online notoriety as the "Star Wars kid." In the video, he is performing an odd ballet as he pretends that he is conducting a mock battle as a Jedi knight. As he swoops and lumbers with the golf club, he creates his own sound effects. Not long after the release, a technologically savvy individual added "Star Wars" sound effects and a movie score.

Ghyslain's movements could come across as either comical or painful to watch as he reenacts his version of a Star Wars battle scene. His performance is, at best, clumsy. At worst, as viewers watch a portly teen flail a golf club, they become voyeurs in a grotesque parody. A viewer may find the latter description to be especially apt when watching one of a dozen cloned and doctored versions of the original—each set to various sounds, from parts of the "Star Wars" soundtrack to rhythmic flatulence.

If Ghyslain had deliberately made this clip public, a viewer might find it funny—perhaps thinking the sequence was an outtake from one of those "funniest home videos" programs. But Ghyslain's short film was not meant for public viewing; it was something he shot privately, a moment caught on tape when he was acting like a silly kid. As the Toronto *Globe and Mail* reported (Ha, 2003), Ghyslain videotaped himself while goofing off in a school video lab. When he finished taping himself, he locked away the tape.

Ghyslain's classmates found the tape and on April 19, 2002, they remastered and uploaded it to the file sharing service KaZaA as a joke. This prank became a nightmare for Ghyslain. Not only did his classmates taunt him for his private act of dorkiness, but the entire world was able to endlessly watch, snicker, giggle, and forward the clip to others. Rather than being Ghyslain's fifteen minutes of fame, the tape gave him endless minutes and years of shame, as the words and images spread across the globe about the Star Wars kid and his gawky light saber dance. For Ghyslain, the emotional trauma of having a private tape available on the Internet became too intense. He dropped out of school and entered a Quebec children's psychiatric ward to finish the academic year.

In 2003, *Wired News* reported that Ghyslain's parents had sued the families of the four boys who had uploaded the private tape. In the suit, they alleged that the classmates stole the tape from a locked cabinet at the private school, then digitized the tape and uploaded it to KaZaA. A *Globe and Mail* reporter covering the lawsuit noted that the classmates attached a note to the clip that asked viewers to make insulting remarks about Ghyslain's performance. The reporter revealed that in the lawsuit's statement of claim, the four classmates not only lacked remorse for uploading Ghyslain's tape, they also attempted to evade school officials' investigations to find the students who were responsible for uploading the tape.

In the lawsuit, Ghyslain's parents claimed that the four classmates' malicious actions turned Ghyslain into an object of scorn and ridicule and resulted in the teenager's need for psychiatric care. In an e-mail interview that appeared in the *National Post*, Ghyslain was quoted as saying, "I want my life back." The worldwide attention and humiliation of a practical joke gone awry is reflected in a statement the *Globe and Mail* published on the filed suit: "Ghyslain had to endure and still endures today, harassment and derision" (Feuer & George, 2005). In April 2006, Raza and his family settled in Canadian court for the minimum sum related to personal damages, C$350,000 (Beaumont, 2006).

As a follow-up to illustrate just how long such an event can occur in cyberspace, three years after the first upload, this young man's embarrassment continues. On December 1, 2006, MSNBC's popular television show *Countdown with Keith Olbermann* announced that Raza's video is considered the "most viral video of all time," with more than 900 million downloads since its debut.

Cautionary Tale #3: William Freund

On October 29, 2005, a nineteen-year-old male with Asperger's syndrome dressed in a black cape and a paintball mask went on a shooting rampage in an affluent neighborhood in Aliso Viejo, California. By the time William Freund finished unloading his twelve-gauge shotgun, he had murdered two people. Then he committed suicide.

Before his attack, William posted his intentions on two websites, wrongplanet.net and SomethingAwful.com. William indicated that he was going to avenge vandalism done the year before to Halloween pumpkins at his home. A CBS News report on November 6, 2005, regarding William's actions quoted a message William posted that he planned to "start a terror campaign to hunt those" who had hurt him. A second post on SomethingAwful.com referred to William staging a Halloween shoot-out "to get even with those who damaged his pumpkins the Halloween a year before." The Associated Press newswire report quoted one response to William's comments: "I can imagine this mongoloid, sitting on his creaky porch, one strap on his overalls, leaping up and running to the defense of his precious 24-ounce pumpkin." Subsequently, William was permanently bounced from the site.

A London *Guardian* report (Hahn, 2005) cited this posting from the SomethingAwful.com website on November 2:

> "Deep breaths, guys," posted Target Practice. "Did we make fun of an autistic kid, tell him where he can find buckshot, then laughed about it? Oh shit." King Hotpants replied: "Yeah, we did. And then he killed people. And himself. I don't think I'm going to sleep tonight." "I told this guy where to get fucking buckshot," wrote Radioactivele.

Information gathered through various news reports revealed that William was a high school graduate who was socially shunned in school. His classmates harassed him, spit on him, and pushed his head into toilets. To find friendship, William turned to the Internet. The Something-Awful.com post above indicated that the online friendships William hoped to find were equally elusive. About a week after the murder-suicide, the Associated Press reported that William posted the following on one of his website profiles: "I've never really had a friend. I've never had someone I can share more intimate conversation with, or just have a good time with" (Associated Press, 2005). Whether in person, on blogs, in chat rooms, or on different websites, William's call for companionship went unanswered. Only three days before the shooting spree, William was bounced from a peer's website for being obnoxious. The Associated Press wire story revealed that William's desire to stage a "Halloween shootout" to get even with pranksters who vandalized his pumpkin the previous Halloween was met with ridicule and the eventual permanent bouncing from the group discussion.

Again, while cyberbullying may not be the sole factor in pushing teenagers to violence, it certainly contributes to the feelings of isolation and loneliness they can have. In particular, these three cases illustrate how boys respond to social isolation and cyberbullying. While cyber attacks also affect adolescent girls, teenage boys may suffer the most from cyberbullying, because unlike girls, they rarely seek help for such abuse.

The British Broadcasting Corporation reported in 2003 that teen boys will search out emotional help for cyberbullying only when they reach a breaking point. Margaret Hodge, then the British minister for children, noted that boys often believe there is no one to turn to in these situations. Girls, it seems, will talk to trusted friends or confide in a parent or teacher if threats become too overwhelming.

Teenage boys rarely ask for help when dealing with cyberbullying because they believe that asking for assistance reinforces the social perception that they are "weak" or not "real men"—boys who need an adult to handle their battles for them (BBC, 2003). Additionally, adults often may not step in and assert control of a potentially violent cyberbullying situation between boys because of the rough-and-tumble quality that boys' friendships often take.

Thomas Newkirk (2002) points out in his book on boys, literacy, and popular culture that the "male code" for friendship frequently carries the expectation that boys tease and share potentially violent actions, such as tussling or playing shooting games. While these actions may seem disturbing to outsiders, the constraints of the male code pressure boys to maintain an appearance of heterosexuality through coarse escapades, aggressive play, cruel jokes, and wit.

But, how far should adults let the male code dominate online discourse before stepping in? While the tendency may be for teachers and parents to let boys be boys, there are certain signs that some male adolescent language and actions may need to be curtailed. For instance, if playful teasing or insulting that is aimed at a wide group (like playing "the dozens") turns to hostility directed solely at a single individual, then adults should consider intervening before the behavior escalates into bullying or violence.

In each of the instances highlighted earlier in this section, teachers or parents could have misread the barbed messages. Thinking that boys will be boys or that the male code was affecting the language of the posts, it is possible that some adults figured the taunting was merely a joke or a set of pranks. Or, in Ghyslain Raza's situation, when school authorities stepped in, perhaps the teenage code of silence was invoked so that no information about what happened emerged from an investigation.

CYBERBULLYING: THE DARK SIDE OF ADOLESCENT LIFE

Although the Internet has brought good things, such benefits are overshadowed when cyberbullying surfaces. At a time when youngsters crave the attention of their peers and strongly desire the elevated power or status that comes with peer acceptance, the effects of social isolation and extreme vulnerability resulting from cyberbullying can wreak havoc on a teenagers' physical, emotional, and mental well-being.

Cyberbullying not only damages the lives of those who are targeted, but also undermines the Internet's potential as an educational tool. According to Ellickson (2000), even well-adjusted teens from financially secure homes can find themselves in dangerous, possibly long-term public health crises like depression, drug use, mental disorders, and violent or unsafe social situations. Some school behaviors, such as cyberbullying, clearly exacerbate the rise and spread of teenage health risks. When two of the leading causes of adolescent morbidity are homicide and suicide (Ellickson, 2000), any aggravating factors that contribute to these deaths need to be examined more closely.

Because cyberspace is created by humans and shaped by human practices, it is a representation of our own lives. Cyberbullying is a reminder that even in virtual space, the teenage years can be very dark and foreboding for some youngsters. Unlike a generation ago, when a prank or practical joke would cause embarrassment for a day or two in school hallways, today, adolescent angst, fears, and humiliation can be magnified by a single keystroke or mouse click—an offending photo, private thought, or detail about a medical condition can be sent multiple times worldwide. Such endless mortification degrades a person, demeans his or her humanity, and shows complete disrespect for the community where the bully lives. If a teenager is already in a personal or emotional crisis, for whatever reason, online bullying worsens or intensifies the teen's problem.

Cyberbullying is a concern for the school and the community. Adults need to find appropriate ways to intervene before these issues become more serious in the middle school years. As I argue in the next chapter, there are a number of possible avenues for prevention that can effectively influence students without being preachy.

Students have been raised in a culture where technology has dominated their lives; they have internalized the warnings. Most know the dangers of putting their private information online, and still, they continue to do so. Concerned adults must ask themselves, why?

Such divulging of private data occurs because blogs have become windows into a blogger's personality and intelligence. Viewers can learn about the blogger's background, personal strengths and interests, preferences on a range of issues or topics, attitudes, anxieties, experiences, dreams, and goals.

Ask any adolescent, and he or she will state without hesitation that the common perception among tweens and teens is that a blog is private, not public, space. Even with all of their technological sophistication, most are incredibly unaware that the Internet is extremely public. Many youngsters believe that if there are items adults do not like on an adolescent's blog, then that's too bad. This view frequently conflicts with teachers' and parents' ideas about what blog content is appropriate for their youngsters' sites.

Still, a third view doesn't have to alienate adults or adolescents. Adults can use disturbing online information to teach rather than to stereotype, to pigeonhole, or to predetermine a student's future. Teachers and parents can use the opportunity to discuss how future college admissions officers or employers—all of whom now take an active role in using blogs to determine whether a teenager is the "right choice" for their institution—make decisions to accept or to hire an applicant based on what online content is displayed.

While students may think trolling personal space is unfair, the reality of the situation cannot be denied. Youngsters will know that their choices to post certain material have consequences. Once they understand how their profiles and posts may influence evaluations of them as future student or employees, they can then make informed decisions as to what material they will post on their blogs.

The good news is that blog content rarely stays constant, so it becomes a barometer for reading students and making educational decisions throughout the school year. However, adults must view students' personal blog spaces with caution: Usually, the student blogger's profile or content is a description that captures a temporary state of mind, for example, a child's feelings on a given day; most adolescents' views change dramatically over the teenage years, and the adults who surround these teens may also hold views that change.

Unless youngsters are engaged in producing content that could harm them or injure others, adults should intervene as little as possible. All too often teenagers in the blogosphere are using blogs to learn more about their worlds—the physical world, the biological world, the social world, and the inner world. Much of the online content is a form of play, or make-believe.

As with fashion, hair care, or cosmetics, teens use online profiles to try on a new identity to see how it fits with their personality. These temporary identities change daily, weekly, or monthly depending on the rate of maturity of a particular individual. The respective behaviors are a way for teens to become autonomous individuals in an increasingly restrictive society.

Adolescents have to make some decisions for themselves regarding how they wish others to perceive them as individuals in society. Adults must realize that sometimes this process may lead to tweens and teens making mistakes in judgment; whether these errors arise from inappropriate blog content or challenging authority at the most inopportune times certainly depends on the teen involved.

However, if the young blogger begins to show signs of bullying, being stalked, or being harassed, adults need to intervene as quickly as possible to ensure that a potential problem does not escalate. Protecting youngsters is a delicate balance; overprotecting adolescents often reflects in creating adults who are afraid to take risks. Teachers and parents need to know the child involved and his or her maturity level to ensure a proper level of protection occurs, regardless of whether the youngster is online or in real life.

7

ENCOURAGING SAFE
BLOGGING PRACTICES

The last chapter highlighted the dark side of teenage blogging. I now want to shift the discussion for the remainder of this book to why blogging can still be an important educational tool and how it can be a valuable classroom activity. Because of the negativity currently surrounding teenage blogging behaviors, discussions on safe blogging frequently focus on sensationalized media stories that overreport the dangers of unsupervised blogging. Such discussions do not address ways of altering the online behaviors of tweens and teens.

The best place to begin this shift is in schools and homes, where educators and parents can introduce students to safe blogging practices. However, encouraging safe blogging practices needs to be a community effort rather than a task left solely to educators or parents to handle. When educators and parents provide children with the proper climate for blogging or for any other Internet-based learning experience, there is no reason why even the youngest students should be excluded from learning in online environments. Of course, such a step requires educators and parents to become far more proficient in new media technologies than many are. Unfortunately, too many adults see computer technology as a simple extension of a more familiar genre—the television.

Plunking kids down for an afternoon of lazy television viewing leads to childhood obesity and self-esteem issues, a lack of engagement in learning, and a strong consumerist or materialist drive, as many educators and parents have discovered over the past few decades. While hours in front of the computer also may lead to childhood obesity, far different issues arise on the Internet. Cyberspace is not television. Educators and parents who fail to recognize the differences between the two media frequently contribute to the problems surrounding both media.

Television, primarily used in American homes as a passive medium or babysitter, seems benign compared to the Internet. While each medium lets strangers with potentially undesirable messages into a home, on a blog or through Instant Messenger, communication is a two-way experience.

In cyberspace, the child is no longer a passive receiver of the messages sent; now the child can have an active role in encouraging or extending the conversations held in cyberspace as often and for as long as the child would like and in a range of electronic genres of the child's own choosing. Moreover, on blogs or in chat rooms, children can create and maintain alternative personas, personalities far different from the ones they display in the classroom or home. Because of their skill with software and computer tools, adolescents can manipulate images, text, and sound to present whatever aspects of their personalities they wish to show the world. Adults have to realize that today's children are digital natives; they are fluent and flexible with new technology in ways that previous generations are not. As digital natives, children have a comfort and skill level that most educators and parents can only hope to imitate.

On the Internet, tweens and teens have an incredible capacity for human agency, the capacity to make choices and to impose their choices on others. For instance, MySpace refers to the user having "my space," a place where someone can write whatever it is he or she wants. Young Internet users often do not understand that even though a blog like MySpace is theirs, it is also a public space, and the words and images presented set up chains of thought that may be misunderstood or misrepresented.

The following real social networking page examples drawn from a headline story in my local paper, the *Philadelphia Inquirer*, highlight this problem:

> "I hate boys, but I sure do LOVE men!" a 17-year-old student from Bucks County (PA) announces in her web log. Keep clicking. You'll see her in pink undies and learn that "pornography" is her hobby. She invites messages from anyone who "likes what they're reading . . ."

For a 15-year-old Gloucester County (NJ) girl, a bikini shot is her greeting card to cyberspace. Admirers are welcome to comment. One asks her to repair his car in the same swimsuit . . .

A 16-year-old in Chester County (PA) had a party while his parents were away. On his web page, friends give him props. One praises the potent weed. One recounts "looking at porn" on the mother's computer. Another raves, "I woke up on the floor 3 times." (Prichard, 2005)

Like dozens of other nationwide news stories on local teenage blogs, this story illustrates Internet choices that are devoid of moral agency, the idea of taking responsibility for one's own words. On the Internet, teenagers have total human agency, or control over their actions and choices for uploading certain material over other items. Yet, many choose not to exercise their moral agency, even though in these types of situations, moral agency is particularly important.

In real life, however, teenagers have a reduced amount of human agency. As they apply value judgments in various daily encounters, they must temper their human agency with moral agency. In classrooms, sports teams, and gangs, appearance matters. When youngsters violate the rules set for them in any of these situations, either overt or subtle punishment occurs. These reprimands teach the youngster what behaviors are appropriate for being part of the group and enforce standards of moral agency that a teen must maintain to remain part of the cohort.

Blogs have no such mechanisms in place to admonish young users for their behaviors. The Internet's philosophy is "you own your own words."

Consequently, encouraging students to engage in safe blogging practices requires adults to actively and regularly promote moral agency. Perhaps youngsters can apply this concept by answering two essential questions whenever they blog: *Should this occur? What can happen if I encourage certain types of behaviors while I'm online?*

This approach would require a significant change in how educators and parents look at children. Rarely in America do adults look at youngsters under eighteen as having the moral agency needed to make critical decisions about their lives. The accessibility of the Internet requires that adults alter this view. When it comes to blogging or to any Internet use where a tween or a teen presents a public persona, educating young users about the significance of what they say about themselves and how others will respond must become part of the school curriculum and parental discussion.

Most of us agree that adolescents have a high degree of technical competence and capability that supersedes the abilities of the adults who surround them. As a result, adults must change the modes for guiding students. Adults who rely upon their own teenage experiences to handle the current social issues and concerns related to blogging and other new media behaviors often create an environment that breeds dismissal or ignorance of the serious effects of these problems. The Internet is not a school playground.

New media technologies change the dimension, scope, and range of influence that bullying, stalking, or other nonsocial behaviors have on adolescents today compared to those of previous generations. Such behaviors were once physical and limited in impact, and so they could be shrugged off or handled later. Because of the tools from today's rich cyberspace environment, harassment has moved beyond school's limits. That change suggests that students who actively engage in cyber abuse choose to do so with a deliberate intent to harm or to exercise their human agency without thinking about its moral component. As a result, many adults must rethink their idea of adolescents as "children being children" when youngsters spend time on blogs, chat rooms, or Instant Messenger. These items are not toys. They are communication tools. Whenever humans use communication tools, there is always an intent and purpose for their use. Whenever there is an intent and purpose, there needs to be moral agency.

The other significant change in looking at youngsters' use of blogs and other cybermedia is that while tweens and teens are digital natives, most adults who surround them are digital immigrants. Teachers, administrators, and parents—even some older brothers and sisters—are still trying to settle into this new technological place. Like any new settler, digital immigrants find themselves in an environment that is already populated by those of a different civilization—children. In what may seem like a cruel twist of fate, today's children push the boundaries of learning and using computer technology. Digital immigrants feel the same way about the Internet as a prior generation of parents felt when television took over American homes.

Such metaphors as "digital natives" and "digital immigrants" aptly describe the foreign experience most adults have when trying to learn more about new technological genres. The ease with which youngsters acclimate to cultural and technological changes is astounding. Still, everyone involved in a child's life must realize this new, different, and important aspect of online communication: Tweens and teens now have an agency, an active role, in these online discussions and practices that has not existed with television or with earlier school practices. For blogging to become a safe educational tool, school personnel, parents, and the community need to develop a more sophisticated understanding of what the preteen and adolescent years are like in the early 21st century to help students make better choices. So much of new media technology is defined by both promise and paradox; blogging, like other new media forms, promises great things. But these promises also bring with them inconsistencies, contradictions, and sometimes illogicalities because humans create and use these technologies. Until society learns how to handle this paradox, the promises seem continually out of reach.

The good news is that the promises that new technologies hold for student learning do not necessarily have to be out of reach. There are ways for children to blog with moral agency in these online genres without sacrificing their human agency and desire to have a public voice.

CAN BLOGGING BE REMEDIED?

It's time to remedy blogging of the social networking stigma that it has received in the mainstream media. Blogging has the potential to become not only an excellent vehicle for enhancing literacy instruction in multiple content areas but also a valuable, enjoyable learning tool for a wide range of students. However, having blogs meet safety and literacy demands requires a multilevel effort from various school groups. In this section, I address how teachers, school administrators, parents, and students have a role to play in recasting blogs as learning instruments rather than mere social networking tools.

Those concerned about safe blogging practices need to focus on discovering the underlying social issues that occur in the classroom or in adolescence that can spread to online environments. Then school officials, parents, and community members need to work with one another to address these concerns or at least provide physical and virtual environments that discourage antisocial behaviors, such as bullying or stalking. Because blogs, like other technologies, are made by humans, they can be controlled by humans. If a community wants its youngsters to have safe, educational blogging experiences, the community has the power to make this happen.

In the following sections, I outline several tips that schools, parents, communities, and students can draw upon to make blogging experiences safer but still enjoyable without students having to sacrifice their personas or identities. Rather than considering these tips as hard-and-fast rules, readers can adopt them as ways for establishing strategies or plans that benefit local school and community needs.

I prefer this approach because a sweeping lockstep model for guiding students' online activities does not take into account the varying pressures and demands different geographic regions have on the learning, cultural, or technological expectations for students. As an educator over the past twenty years, I have found that the most productive policies come from local control rather than from imposition from above. Thinking about these tips as proposals for implementation in a given school allows everyone in the district, whether administrators, teachers, students, parents, or community leaders, to voice their views and to come to a consensus.

While I start with the school community, because that is where most of the concerns lie, I also address tips that should be deliberated in other affected groups as well. If there is any universal bit of advice to be offered, it is that blogging is a form of free speech, and students should not be barred from engaging in this type of discourse. Regardless of students' religious views, race, politics, sexuality, or cultural backgrounds, teenagers require and deserve outlets where they can speak freely about the issues that concern them. My goal here is to provide the means for youngsters to feel safe when voicing their worries and interests.

FIVE TIPS FOR SCHOOLS

Schools are at the center of the debate swirling around adolescents who are blogging. Even though many of the problems linked to students and blogging happen off campus and after the school day, everyone realizes that eventually these issues find their way to the school. Because some of these problems have extremely serious effects in schools, more than a few administrators have taken to rooting around teenagers' personal blogs and diaries as a way to protect the school's interests. Rather than taking the Big Brother approach to students' blogs or online journals, a more proactive model may be for schools to follow these tips for making blogging safer for students:

1. Offer workshops to students on proper blogging practices.
2. Set up regular workshops with medical and behavioral professionals as well as a cohesive peer mediation system to deal with adolescent problems, depression, risky behaviors, and school or academic difficulties.
3. Consider using only classroom-friendly blog hosting sites on school grounds and letting parents know that these sites have been "school approved."
4. Create common experiences in schools connected to Internet use.

Offer Student Workshops on Proper Blogging Practices

Preteens and teens are invincible, at least in their own minds. Very few of them know or believe that someone might be out there waiting to harm them physically or emotionally. Most youngsters think everyone is a friend or a potential friend.

This lack of judgment comes from tweens' and teens' innate desire to be wanted and loved. Youngsters think others mirror them or who they wish to be. The social pull on tweens and younger teens is great; even level-headed kids can make some really absurd decisions when they are trying to be someone they are not.

As more educators are learning, many cyberbullying and cyberstalking issues begin long before students reach middle school. The behaviors that culminate in bullying or stalking online begin in students as young as nine years old. This is why yearly workshops that teach students in the fourth grade and up about responsible blogging and Internet usage are becoming critical for preventing future problems. In fourth grade, most students are able to reason, read, and write fairly well, and some students may be entering a socially aggressive stage in their lives.

Similar to the "sex ed" talks given to students back in the 1960s and 1970s, these workshops might be better conducted in a same-gender setting. Particular problem issues that emerge in blogging, like sexual harassment or abusive language, can be more delicately handled in single-gender groupings. So too can certain issues of personal tolerance and recognition, such as sexual mores, behaviors, or practices. Because many of the problems adolescents face are highly personal in nature, students may feel more comfortable speaking about how cyberbullying affects them if they are not in a heterogeneous group.

As students enter the later middle school or early high school years, more sensitive issues like online dating or chat room predators can be addressed. Schools might want to bring professional speakers, perhaps local police officials, social workers, or medical staff, to discuss delicate problems that arise from risky behaviors when students blog without thinking about the consequences of their postings.

The focus on talking to students about these concerns reflects a change in the way educators and parents need to view their children's lives. As many of the cases presented earlier in this book have shown, parents may be providing the proper educational, social, and religious instruction in the home, but their children might still be posing on MySpace or LiveJournal or some other blogging site as a gangsta, a pimp, a player, or a sexually active teenager.

Implementing safe blogging practices means more than telling students not to put their personal information out into cyberspace. Teacher and parent discussions also need to cover personal responsibility online and the need for bloggers to think about how readers may respond to posted material. If a child writes in a sexually suggestive way, for instance, readers may conclude that the writer is promiscuous, a situation that may put the child in danger. Likewise, if a teen posts several messages about excessive indulgence in alcohol or drugs, visitors may think that the teen is an alcoholic or a drug user. Because colleges and employers now scour MySpace and other social networking spaces for this data, such information can endanger future university or work opportunities for teenagers. Teens need to be made aware of how others may respond to their words and act accordingly.

Respect is a central theme in adolescent behavior, whether it is maintaining respect or retaliating against someone who "disrespects" a friend or a teen. Teachers need to explain to students that spreading malicious gossip, rumor, and falsehoods leads to a loss of respect not only for the victim but also for the attacker.

Part of developing safe blogging practices for the classroom means that teachers, school administrators, parent representatives, and student government representatives need to set rules for blogging in schools. Educational psychologists have argued for years that teenagers want boundaries and rules, as long as they have some say in generating the policies. There is no reason for schools not to hold workshops and meetings that encourage parents and students to participate in creating school rules for safe blogging since there is so much overlap of rules between the school and home when tweens and teens blog. It is important for educators and parents to take the lead in helping students set the norms for safe blogging behaviors.

In many of the instances that have garnered media coverage, it is clear that neither the school staff nor the parents knew what the students were doing. When probed further, it was equally clear that the students had no idea what they were getting themselves into. Having clear, well-defined, and uniform policies for blogging on school grounds helps administrators, teachers, and parents be proactive rather than reactive. Adults often forget that students frequently appreciate boundaries for appropriate behaviors, since many are unsure how to adapt their social skills to a virtual environment. This does not mean schools and parents should set draconian rules; rather, school staff and parents need to determine—in conjunction with student leaders—what language is acceptable and what topic areas represent a student's individuality but also meet a community's standards.

Set Up Peer Mediation Workshops with Local Health-Care Workers

At the heart of cyberbullying lie a number of social conflicts. Cyberbullying is the result of a series of mishandled, unconstructive, or ignored social problems in schools and neighborhoods. Rather than allowing students to use the Internet to "solve" their issues with others, schools may find it more constructive to have students attend monthly voluntary workshops on peer mediation led by local health-care workers.

Rather than focusing on discovering who is right or wrong in these workshops, students can work with area medical and behavioral professionals to discover ways of telling their stories and expressing their views without treating others with disrespect. Students can learn how to move beyond immediate social conflicts to find ways of solving relationship problems that do not result in verbal, physical, or emotional abuse.

Peer mediation works best for reducing the root causes that frequently lead to school violence: name-calling, rumor-spreading, and aggressive physical behaviors, like bumping in hallways and physical intimidation. While teachers and school administrators can use peer mediation approaches to address specific issues, the mediation process functions better when students become trained as peer mediators and hold regular class meetings and workshops with local professionals.

Peer mediation programs work well with middle school students, for instance, when the effort and commitment come primarily from students rather than parents or school staff. Student peer mediators frequently act as role models for students' behaviors, and they take the lead in encouraging students to talk out their problems or concerns before acting upon them. Harnessing peer influence for lowering the heat and intensity of many social conflicts is critical for avoiding trouble outside of the school. Because trained student peer mediators learn not to judge or take sides in a story, they become important voices of reason. More important, because trained student peer mediators work with students to come to a quick resolution, the affected students do not have to dwell upon their feelings or stew in their emotions—two reasons why students resort to cyberbullying to solve a relationship problem.

When combined with other ideas presented in this chapter, peer mediation has the potential to stave off the social conflicts that give rise to most instances of cyberbullying. Adults need to remember that even though adolescents may look and sound like they are mature, many are not emotionally literate. In fact, most are trying to come to terms with their shifting emotions. A well-done peer mediation program can help students learn emotional literacy skills that prompt them to think about how their behaviors and reactions can lead to unintended or undesired consequences when or if they engage in cyberbullying.

Consider "Classroom-Friendly" Sites for Student Access

One of the best things about new media technology is that it allows people access to hundreds of possible outlets where they can find whatever they need. Teachers can easily find blogging tools that are classroom friendly. Not all classroom-friendly blogging tools have to be connected to an expensive software package like BlackBoard. Some excellent blog sites exist that are free for classroom use and offer a safe environment for students to focus on their learning.

While I do not endorse any particular site over another, three blog hosting sites for classroom use that are frequently named in articles are www.21publish.com/classroom, www.classblogmeister.com, and www.chalksite.com. Each site is well-known in the "edublogging" field as being reputable and safe for classroom use.

In selecting a blog hosting site for the classroom, teachers should examine the skills and time needed for them to develop a blog. To create a useful educational blog for the classroom, teachers must invest some skill and time in learning the material. School administrators thinking of onsite workshops for teachers should consider a series of weekly workshops throughout a semester with a skilled education-based blogger to guide teachers through the various stages of classroom blogging.

Most college or university writing or English programs have a computer and writing specialist or two on staff who can work with K–12 or K–13 teachers in both the technical and pedagogical aspects of blogging with students. Since 2001, college faculty have been incorporating blogging into college writing courses, and there is a wealth of knowledge available to local school districts that tap into their nearby university faculties for this information. For schools that are near a National Writing Project site, a technology liaison is usually available for consultation and workshops with area teachers as well.

Implementing safe blogging practices does not have to be a drain on school coffers. With free blog hosting sites, local experts can guide novice teachers and teachers who have the desire to incorporate more technology into their classes. Students' adventures in blogging can make the local news—albeit for the right reasons.

Create Common Experiences in Schools Related to Internet Use

Schools are filled with common experiences that bond the students together as a cohesive community: proms, pep rallies, service learning, and graduation are but a few events that resonate as common points of contact. Still, other common experiences can also help students form a community that resists cyberbullying:

- Language
- Kinship
- Music
- Extracurricular activities
- Exams

When students pull together, whether through shared language or shared emotions surrounding the SAT, they get to know each other as people rather than isolated cliques. All the items listed above create a sense of ritual about being in school that pushes students beyond the early learned rituals of home and family. Students who lack home and family rituals often look to schools to provide that sense of trust in the community that is missing outside of the classroom. When schools fail to instill trust in the community, tweens and teens sometimes turn to gangs, violence, or early sexual relations to find a sense of missing community.

However, it takes more than student participation in various social or athletic activities to shape a school community. Students can also form a community when they learn together. Forming school rituals that relate to use of the Internet, particularly blogs, can be a successful method for bridging the school-cyberspace connections that occur.

To initiate common experiences with blogging in the classroom, teachers can create a number of shared assignments where students must work collaboratively. Colleges and universities often have common assignments that all students taking a course have to complete. The idea behind the common assignment is to provide a shared learning experience that generates a learning community in a course or grade level.

To ensure that these assignments become a common experience for students, every classroom for students in the same grade level would undertake the same unit at some point in the school year. Depending on the classroom structure and teacher preparation, a teacher for one grade level might stagger the experience across the academic year, while a teacher for another grade level might focus on the same unit for an entire marking period. How a school constructs the common experience requires the administration and faculty to look at a number of local school variables, such as block scheduling, year-round class attendance, student ability, and the appropriate grade level for offering such an assignment.

TYPES OF COMMON CLASS ASSIGNMENTS

Once administrators and teachers set the local criteria and the parameters for the shared learning experience, they can decide on what type of common assignment they will use:

- The research blog
- The technology autobiography blog
- Web quests or other guided discovery projects that can be blogged

Each task offers teachers not only the opportunity to encourage collaborative work but also the prospect for promoting both writing and electronic communication across the curriculum.

These blog activities set the stage for experiential learning, the type of hands-on tasks that many students enjoy and learn from. Because the construction and maintenance of a blog can be quite time consuming, students with varying abilities and talents complement each other and thus work well together. Groups are also more productive because a person in a group has the chance to be more engaged than he or she might be in the larger classroom.

The Research Blog

A research blog can be used in science or math classes with ease. Teams of students are able to write down their observations and create laboratory reports that other classmates can use to replicate an experiment, just as research in science or math is conducted in real life. Students can write about their ideas, results, discoveries, failures, and opinions about a given research task. Those students who want to supplement their findings can link to science blogs where other similar or more extensive research and experiments are being conducted.

On the research blog, students who have artistic skills can produce specific graphics or images that help others learn more about what the students are learning in the laboratory or classroom. Students who are more language-oriented can write or edit the content to make it clearer for the average reader. A research blog offers an opportunity for students of each gender to discover more about the research process and see its larger connection to learning science and math. For teenage girls in particular, learning about science through blogging may encourage young women to explore science in college or as a career. Some girls might be attracted to journaling to record the daily life of a scientist, while other girls might find the idea of blogging on current scientific developments a good way to connect with class material.

Similarly, the research blog can be set up for literature, history, and foreign language classes. In these classes, where girls often excel, boys may find themselves excluded from discussions. When teenage boys learn about literature and foreign language through blogging, they may discover ideas that help them perform better in class.

The blog can be as extensive and robust as students wish it to be, which makes it a very adaptable writing and research tool for middle school and high school classrooms. Depending upon a student's interest, a blog is flexible enough to accommodate a range of topics. And, of course, for those mainstream or inclusion classes, teachers can take note: Regardless of whether a student is a special needs or a traditional learner, there is a place for any type of learner in a research blog group. That means every student can work together and offer something to the group.

The Technology Autobiography Blog

What would be more fun to write about . . . what I did on my summer vacation (again) or why do I use the technological gadgets that surround me? My undergraduate students love writing about their technological literacy—or lack thereof. As they trace their technology usage, my students often discover interesting patterns about their learning and interests. In the process of writing about their own technology experiences, students unearth a number of fascinating cultural artifacts or moments that turn what could have been a simple personal essay into a phenomenological inquiry about their relationship to machines.

The technology autobiography blog is a "meta" approach to students thinking about their information and technology literacy. As they write their technology histories, students are focusing on writing for a public audience (their classmates) and how their experiences fit in with others. When students write these autobiographical blogs in groups, they talk with each other to shape their narratives and represent the entire group's adventures with technology. Students also learn about history and current events by linking their experiences to the world at large.

Teachers who are concerned about grading a research blog can find guidelines on the Internet for evaluating student blogs. Using the online guidelines as a framework, a teacher can produce something that is specific for his or her classroom needs and student population. And, if the school uses one of the classroom-friendly blog hosting sites, students are safe from uninvited guests joining the discussions.

The Guided Discovery Blogs

Nowadays web quests are fairly common activities in middle school. Students take a topic and research it in a scavenger hunt-like manner, searching out questions and data. As a guided discovery task, web quests help engage students in online research. Students begin to learn how to make choices and address problem solving in a creative fashion. This is a fine first step in helping students develop computer skills; however, web quests are only a rudimentary stage in building students' technology literacy.

There are other avenues for guided discovery assignments that teachers can use to show students how to blog for academic purposes. Here are three examples of guided discovery tasks that can be used across the curriculum:

- Word-of-the-day blog (vocabulary building)
- Reading journal blog
- Grammar blog

While many language arts teachers will find these activities very useful, all teachers have vocabulary, reading, and grammar issues to address in class. A blog makes these topics more interactive and relevant for students.

Word-of-the-Day Blog. Whether they are learning language arts, math, or science, students must know particular vocabulary words to ensure they have a firm grasp of certain concepts. The word-of-the-day blog encourages students to post a new vocabulary word from the previous night's assignment.

Besides offering the working definition of the term, students should be able to cross-reference the word with any of its other meanings in other academic subjects, provide links to web pages that explain the concept in greater depth, and insert graphics or sound where appropriate.

A hands-on connection to vocabulary is important for students in all classes. However, where there may be the most growth and development is with English as a Second Language (ESL) students, who can practice idiomatic or colloquial uses, make connections between English and their home language, and practice their technology skills. Many times, teachers are unsure how to help ESL students build or improve their literacy, especially if these students are in their later teenage years. The word-of-the-day blog can become an important teaching tool for these situations, and it can function in a way that does not isolate language learners from the mainstream student population.

Reading Journal Blog. Everyone has heard the criticism that secondary school students just do not read enough. Whether the complaint comes from the news media, college professors, parents, cranky teaching colleagues, or industry leaders, the protests ring loud and clear throughout society. With all the electronic choices students have around them, leisurely reading takes a back seat to those activities that seem less draining, like blogging, podcasting, or Instant Messaging.

Instead of forcing students to read, educators and parents have to think more creatively. Having students set up reading journal blogs to share their views on books assigned in class encourages students not only to read the works but to write about the ideas in the books. Students can visit their peers' blogs and leave comments about the poster's opinions or discussion about the reading.

Teachers will have to instruct students on appropriate language to use for a public journal, because students sometimes try to take advantage of language misuse by sneaking in clever acronyms or abbreviations. A teacher workshop on current student slang and acronymic use can be of great help for those teachers who might feel underprepared to discuss this issue with students.

Grammar Blog. Grammar is an area that students forget all too quickly. Many of my college students cannot remember the last time they had any grammar instruction; those who do remember place the moment somewhere in eighth grade. Without regular, sustained practice in the use of correct grammar through writing, it is not hard to understand why high school and college students do not remember the last time they learned anything related to sentence structure, usage, or mechanics.

Teachers frequently say they don't have time or the ability to teach grammar, but truthfully, many teachers do not know the grammar rules either. And, as most people know, if a teacher does not know a subject area well, he or she probably won't focus on the topic very much. Also, when compared to literature, which many teachers find exciting because they are avid readers, grammar is shunned because it is perceived by everyone in the class as boring.

Perhaps a blog might help with grammar. Combined with blogging, grammar might not be as boring as one might first think. A grammar blog can become a communal gaming site where students can engage in some friendly competition—either in teams or individually. Here's how such a grammar gaming blog might work:

In class, students are given four sentences, three of which are incorrect. On their blogs, students have to explain why the three sentences they selected as incorrect are, indeed, incorrect. Of course, students can use their grammar books for reference. Teachers and classmates then visit the sites and leave comments as to the veracity of the student's claims. At the end of each week, the teacher posts the correct answers and praises those students who did well on their grammar.

As students move from grade level to grade level, teachers can refine their grammar blogs. Issues of style, citations, and other technical items can be presented on a grammar blog when students master the basic concepts. For those students who struggle with grammar, the blog can provide a tutorial. Students can return to the blog for thorny problems they have with punctuation, homonyms, or other irksome language issues. Students who excel in grammar instruction can become peer tutors and teach others who may need a little extra help.

These communal assignments focus on having students mix with their peers. Students learn to value the ideas and beliefs of their classmates. For younger teens, this experience can be an important way of reducing some of the social conflicts that lead to cyberbullying or other emotionally abusive behaviors found on blogs or Instant Messenger.

PARENTS ENCOURAGING SAFE BLOGGING

As I mentioned earlier in this chapter, schools alone cannot be expected to address the current problems on MySpace sites or other student blogs. Parents also have a role to play in curbing cyberbullying or other harassing behaviors in online environments.

In a Pew Internet study, Lenhart, Madden, and Hitlin (2005) found that 62 percent of parents make random online checks of their children's MySpace accounts. Even so, probably a significant number of those adults fail to realize that many tweens and teens have multiple MySpace accounts—one for Mom, Dad, and the teachers to see, and one for friends. Often, as some of my graduate students have learned when stumbling across nieces', nephews', students', or younger siblings' second MySpace account, the two sites are extremely different. Linda, a graduate student in my Writing for Electronic Communities class, said, "I'm not sure which person is in front of me—the sweet niece I know or the nasty girl on her MySpace profile" (personal correspondence, February 27, 2006).

Because students create multiple sites with very dissimilar profiles, parents and guardians have to allow for the possibility that their tweens and teens could have diverse personalities. Rather than be shocked, disappointed, or disgusted by the content on the "not for parents and teachers" MySpace site, adults need to have serious discussions with their adolescents as to why they feel the need to put disturbing content on their MySpace account. While many youngsters upload certain photos or material purely for shock value, some are seeking attention, acceptance, or recognition from others. Parents need to determine whether their children are simply trying to push the envelope of bad taste or whether esteem issues are driving their choices to promote troubling images or profiles.

Beyond regular conversations with tweens and teens about their Internet usage, parents have to pay closer attention to where and when their children are online and what they are doing. Authorities agree that those under eighteen years old should have some adult supervision when online; adults should generally make sure the computer is in a well-traveled area of the home. The reason for this guideline is because many of the more alarming stories of cyberbullying, stalking, and MySpace sites come from those adolescents who have a computer and online access in a private part of the house, like a bedroom or isolated section of a basement.

Blogging and other Internet activities are fun and can be excellent tools for learning, but tweens and teens need some parental guidance as to when they should be online. Many children log onto their MySpace or other blog accounts after school and stay there throughout the evening. Seven or more hours of blogging a day is unhealthy, both physically and mentally. Here's what I mean: if children blog seven hours a day (let's say from 3 PM until 10 PM), seven days a week, that's forty-nine hours a week—the equivalent time a person would spend in a full-time job. Add in any extra time students might spend blogging while at school or on their cell phones, and some tweens and teens may be blogging nearly sixty hours a week.

Limiting children to two hours a day of blogging time five or six days a week allows students to have plenty of time to communicate on their blogs, update blog material, and do any necessary schoolwork expected on a blog. Blogging ten to twelve hours a week allows students time for other activities, such as playing sports, doing paper-based homework, volunteering, or taking instrument lessons. Tweens and teens who strike a good balance between blogging and other events in their lives have less opportunity to cyberbully and healthier, more productive channels for their energy.

With all the media warnings, an increasing number of parents may be ensuring that their children blog under adult supervision. But, these actions still may not be enough. How children blog is also important for parents to examine. As Linda, the graduate student I referred to earlier in this chapter, noted, "I can't understand the language these kids use—it's like it's in code. . . . I mean, I'm only thirty, and I can't figure out what they're saying. I feel so old." Here is an example of what Linda could have read on her niece's MySpace account:

YT?
PLZ POS BBL
WE

The standard written English transcription of this exchange reads:

You there?
Please, parent over shoulder. Be back later.
Whatever.

Like all forms of language, blog speak is a type of code. Digital natives are fluent; interlopers or immigrants are not. And adults, even thirty-year-old adults, frequently are interlopers or immigrants. Usually, adults have to learn IM Speak, or Instant Message Speak, the blog code for teens. Luckily, there are many places on the web that have IM Speak lexicons, and there are even computer software programs that translate IM Speak into English.

While it's fine and necessary for adolescents to have their own language—after all, Pig Latin and slang are two generational types of coded teen language—parents should become familiar with the basic acronyms and emoticons used in Instant Message. A simple Google search for "IM speak" can yield several updated locations on the web. Cracking the code for blog speak offers great insight into what some students are thinking and writing about, even when supervision is present.

TWEENS AND TEENS CREATING SAFE BLOGGING SPACES

It would be remiss for anyone to say that users of blogs have no responsibility in creating safe blogging spaces. If any group should have the greatest influence in this matter, it should be the youngsters themselves. They are the more skilled users; they too have the most to lose if unsafe or antisocial behaviors dominate the blogosphere.

While school summits on cyberbullying or harassment often help, students don't always listen to the messages in these meetings. Similarly, with groups like Parry Aftab's TeenAngels, an anti-bullying peer advice team, some students are not receptive to the message. These tweens and teens need more direction in helping them stay safe and not harm others in the blogosphere.

Adolescents must understand that without their participation in curbing cyberbullying, stalking, or other online predatory behaviors, these problems can grow exponentially. While schools and communities should offer workshops, conferences, and seminars for children and their parents, blog users have to become vigilant about their own protection.

Endless repetition of messages about keeping passwords, pictures, and personal information private sometimes generates message fatigue in teenagers' minds. If these users haven't been affected at some point by a cyber abuser, they forget about the risks and may divulge their private information online. A more effective approach may be one that requires students to role-play various scenarios on how to handle privacy issues in workshops, at summits, or in classrooms.

Responsible blog use should become part of the school curriculum. Being a good citizen on the Internet involves learning how to use the available tools. There is no reason why students can't have poster contests, safety seminars, or other workshops they hold that focus on the following points of responsible blogging:

Walk away and discard. Instead of firing off a nasty response, student bloggers should walk away from the computer for a few minutes, do something else, and then process the message. Then they can discard the mean-spirited or disrespectful message upon returning to the computer.

Use the available tools. Students should fight the urge to fire back by hitting Delete, blocking the sender's e-mail address from their computer, and setting filters to eliminate poison posts. If harassing posts still make their way through to the computer, they can use monitoring software or save copies on the hard drive to use as evidence of harassment. As weird as it might seem, students should Google their names often. It's not an ego trip to check what others might be saying. If a student's name is showing up in unwanted places, Google has a tool for removing the offending information. Students can always access current Google tool software by visiting the Google home page and clicking on Help or Tools.

If the texting or blog posts are too much of a burden, let a trusted adult know. A family friend, a close cousin, aunt or uncle, a religious leader, a physician or counselor, a teacher, or any adult who has some perspective on life can be a great ally in this situation. There are many options for action besides retaliation and escalation of a flame war. Students would be wise to let cooler (and sometimes older) heads prevail.

What is important to teach adolescents is that the old saying used in school, "Don't get mad—get even," is the worst approach for stopping cyber abuse. In the blogosphere, revenge is not sweet; it escalates the problem. Tweens and teens who treat their peers with disrespect need help, not fuel. By showing students how to incorporate moral agency along with human agency, adults empower youngsters to discover positive ways for taking control of these situations.

COMMUNITIES ENCOURAGING SAFE BLOGGING

Safe blogging for adolescents is a community problem. Libraries, teen centers, and civic organizations should be holding workshops and seminars to educate parents and others as to what can be done to help children blog without harassment. Far too often, however, community involvement usually means police intervention, such as a sting or a covert operation to surf MySpace pages for illegal activity.

While police scrutiny may be necessary at times to stop known predators or criminals from harming minors, such an approach for monitoring most teens' use of blogs seems heavy-handed and might encourage some students to give officers "something to look for" in their searches. Community seminars held with student leaders or respected local representatives or key communicators tend to be proactive and better designed to change youngsters' behaviors.

Community leaders working with parent-teacher groups or school administrators can provide off-campus discussions that may resonate better with some student populations. Whether they are local mental health counselors, medical professionals, or area luminaries whom students admire, sometimes voices not affiliated with schools can make a difference in sending the same messages educators send to students. The goal for encouraging safe blogging is widespread education about blogs, about their potential for enhancing learning, and about responsible use.

A FINAL NOTE

Tweens and teens need a place to be themselves. Adolescents have to find those spots where they can develop their personalities. Blogging offers such an environment for preteens and teenagers alike.

Encouraging safe blogging should not be about censorship, a lack of trust, or constant monitoring of students' behaviors. Rather, to promote healthy blogging environments, schools, parents, and community organizations need to develop paradigms and programs that reduce relational aggression in younger students, educate children about keeping personal information private, and shape students' perceptions of what physical and psychological safety are in the real world and online. Adults have to help youngsters discover proactive ways of blogging safely rather than firing off reactive posts or retaliatory messages.

Blogs, like any technological medium, are only as useful as humans make them. If educators and parents want their children to have safe blogging spaces, then it becomes critical to teach youngsters how to prevent or turn away from behaviors like direct social control over others

("You can't be my friend unless . . ."), social alienation or isolation (silencing or excluding students from activities), or all-out rejection (mongering rumors, denying a child's presence, and so on). These lessons must be taught before middle school, however. As some studies have indicated (Crick, Casas, & Ku, 1999; Nelson, Robinson, & Hart, 2005), children as young as three years old can display relational aggressive behavior.

The effect that relationally aggressive behavior has on activities in and out of school is why safe blogging practices are a community issue. A blog is merely the latest outlet for covert aggression. Schools, parents, and social service organizations need to form coalitions and alliances to prevent covert relational aggression in children before it takes hold in schools, at home, and in the town or city. Blogging should not be banned in schools, but the undesirable social behaviors in the blogosphere should be.

A concerted community effort can remediate blogs and bring the medium into the schools as a critical communication and learning tool. Blogs are a genre par excellence for designing learning that is innate, unprompted, and autonomous. Blogs offer students and teachers the opportunity to initiate dialogues between school and world perspectives as well as encourage multiple levels of participation from all students. In addition, blogs can break down the barriers between learning in school and learning in the real world, so students can see how their ideas play out in society. Last, for an increasing number of students who are facile with technology, blogs combine experience with excitement in the learning process.

In a remediated setting, blogs can be a learning laboratory that welcomes all students. Encouraging students to take responsibility for safe blogging practices is where remediation begins.

INTEGRATING MULTIPLE INTELLIGENCES AND BLOGGING

The last few chapters focused on social and relational issues connected to blogging in school settings. While these concerns are very important, equally significant is how to turn blogging into an academic activity. Previously, I said that encouraging students to engage in safe blogging practices is the first step in remediating the negative perception of blogging as a mere social networking tool. In this chapter, I move the discussion forward by showing educators and parents why incorporating blogging into the academic curriculum can enhance various forms of learning and critical thinking.

When students blog, different kinds of thinking processes occur compared to when they write using more traditional academic forms. As educational psychologist Howard Gardner has noted extensively in his work on multiple intelligences, thinking critically in these newer domains often depends upon fresh or unique approaches. Special, unusual, or diverse information transfers happen when students encounter new areas and must apply their knowledge in different ways.

There is a perception in some educational and political circles that writing and thinking are transferable skills. I tend to disagree. For any skill to be truly transferred, the contexts in which the abilities or competencies are passed on must be the same. Genuinely transferable writing and thinking, then, requires that context A and context B are identical so proficiency can be determined. The difficulty is that English classes differ in content and purpose from math or science classes, and academic writing is often at odds with workplace writing, journalistic writing, or creative writing. A student writer who is talented or proficient in one type of writing may not be as competent in another type of writing.

A student's lack of writing ability in different fields should not be taken to mean that a learner is inept, unskilled, or educationally disadvantaged, the usual complaints issued when students have problems applying critical writing or thinking abilities to new situations. Fluctuations in student writing can occur because some students' intelligence domains are stronger in other realms than the logico-linguistic sphere. The key is to find assignments and learning environments that not only build upon students' dominant multiple intelligences but also strengthen their weaker competencies. In such a process, students discover how to generate portable—that is, easy to convert or designed to be used from context to context—writing and thinking skills that match their cognitive and learning patterns.

Educators and parents need to realize that to build portable competencies in students' writing and thinking, learners have to compose multiple, lengthy, and varied texts. To instill critical writing and thinking skills that students can integrate as expected in various contexts, teachers and administrators must establish transdisciplinary approaches to literacy.

Blogging can be a coherent method for teaching students writing and thinking skills in ways that align their tacit knowledge, their current ability level, and the school's curricular standards. When done well, classroom blogging can raise teachers', students', and parents' expectations that all learners be able to handle complex or challenging course material. Several longitudinal studies, such as the one conducted by Thomas and Collier in 1997, indicate that interactive learning as well as discovery learning activities help students achieve more in their lessons.

In the blogosphere, students learn how to work with numerous properties of language and image. As a result, the abilities required for most blog-based linguistic and visual manipulations exceed those used in ordinary expository writing tasks performed in school. For instance, when students generate metaphors and avatars for their blogs, or they drift into expressive writing, they blend aesthetics with linguistic intelligence. Additionally, as students select the content for their blogs, they develop a high level of discrimination in choosing online content and can address real world issues they find relevant. Such activities enhance critical thinking by encouraging students to participate in interesting and meaningful work, as opposed to the busy work many students face in lower level or non-college-track high school classes.

Other significant intelligences are addressed through blogging. As student writers build their blogs, they discover how to integrate spatial intelligence with linguistic and artistic intelligence. Should they decide to incorporate audioblogging, podcasting, or music in their blogs, then they learn how to integrate musical intelligence. Throughout the creation of a blog, students develop their kinesthetic intelligence as they hone physical keyboarding skills, hand-eye coordination, and other motor capacities to ensure the blog works properly.

In this mode of thinking, student bloggers make choices about and set purposes for their blogs based on personal and cultural decisions that encourage critical thinking in a practical context. During the creation of a blog, student writers have to make consequential judgments, evaluations, and assessments about what material is appropriate in a given context. As a result, blogs offer writing and literacy opportunities where students can demonstrate their range of intelligence beyond the usual means of psychometric study or standardized testing.

What should excite teachers and parents, and what certainly stimulates students, about the blogging process is how differences across gender, racial, and ability groups can be redistributed in a classroom. Students can draw upon their intelligence in ways that correspond to their thinking processes, regardless of whether they prefer interpersonal communication or logical-mathematical-spatial tasks.

Moreover, what seems to motivate students to blog centers on a single issue: leadership. All student bloggers have an opportunity to be leaders, people who can change another's thoughts, feelings, or behaviors, through the words and images they put on their blogs. As Howard Gardner (1999) notes, voluntary leaders—those who motivate others to change without coercion—are able to guide through storytelling. More important, however, is that the stories voluntary leaders tell are grounded in their own lives. If educators and parents look more closely at MySpace or other blogging sites, they will discover that tweens and teens are trying to direct their own lives (and perhaps the lives of others) through the stories they tell.

Everything from the profiles students create to the diary entries they post suggests that adolescent bloggers attempt to frame events and situations to encourage readers to think in their own ways about the world and their place in it. Gardner indicates that dramatic stories about lives of individuals, as well as details about their families and significant members, draw readers into the narrative. As readers enter these familiar settings, they begin to identify with the blogger and start to share common causes.

While many adolescents' blog postings seem banal to teachers, parents, or other adults, a good number of these stories are special for other tweens and teens. For adults, the blog posts are too familiar and trite, mostly oft-repeated tales of teenage angst that hold no significance in adult lives. But for regular readers of teen blogs, the entries weave narratives that ring true. Such narrative authenticity in blogging arises from three distinct intelligences:

- Exceptional linguistic intelligence that allows for skillful writing and storytelling abilities
- Strong interpersonal intelligence that taps into others' desires, fears, hopes, and emotions
- Excellent intrapersonal intelligence in that the blogger has a well-developed awareness of his or her personal strengths, weaknesses, and goals

Successful adolescent bloggers contribute stories that mirror daily life for other tweens and teens. They speak directly and simply to their peers, sometimes interweaving symbols of their time—music, icons, images, logos, and so forth. At times, these bloggers challenge authority or risk their reputations by posting particular messages or profiles.

Through their iconoclastic behaviors, teenage bloggers practice what Howard Gardner (1993) calls "the intelligences of creators and leaders." Rather than engaging teachers, parents, or other adults in argument, adolescents use blogs to show how irrelevant their elders are. Because so many young bloggers are highly talented and intelligent individuals, it is not too hard to see how persuasive some of them can be to other bloggers or peers. Compared to their experiences in school, when these youngsters are online, their scope of power changes and grows exponentially. Initially, these often sardonic or satirical bloggers address teens who share similar life experiences and technological ability.

As the blog's popularity increases and more readers come aboard, the blogger is able to change readers' ideas, so others begin to make decisions based upon what they read on a youngster's blog. Consequently, teenage bloggers who develop popular sites are, in effect, key communicators—opinion leaders or shapers—acting in leadership roles.

This is why moral agency is crucial in shaping adolescent intelligence. Because large numbers of tweens and teens offer advice on blogs, or at a minimum are the blogosphere's opinion leaders, they need to temper their thoughts with wisdom.

Howard Gardner (1993, 1999) argues that those who are able to draw upon several multiple intelligences simultaneously are more likely to be perceived as wiser than those who cannot. The reason for this, Gardner observes, is that a person who can access a greater number of abilities for making an evaluation appears to be wise. Likewise, if teens who blog can articulate life lessons or express their thoughts at a deeper level, people tend to view them as wiser compared to other teenagers.

MULTIPLE INTELLIGENCE THEORY AND BLOGGING

There is no such thing as *multiple intelligence blogging*, and to argue for something along those lines is pointless. Those who study multiple intelligence theory realize that ideas, practices, and behaviors are not goals or ends for learning in themselves. Rather, multiple intelligence theory presents concepts for generating an educational environment that promotes ranges of human creativity, mental representations, and physical abilities.

Blogs are an exceptional educational tool for incorporating multiple intelligence theory in the classroom because blogs contain markers or characteristics that are hospitable for initiating compatible multiple intelligence practices. The following (adapted from Gardner, 1993) is a short list of characteristics that appear in schools where multiple intelligence theory has had success:

- A school culture that supports diverse learners and encourages steady, hard work

- A school culture that already shares a philosophy aligned in some way with multiple intelligence theory
- A school culture where collaboration occurs at a number of stages or levels in the learning process
- A school culture where curriculum and assessment are meaningful and are grounded in various flexible options for gauging student growth and learning
- A school culture dedicated toward encouraging high-quality student work
- A school culture where the arts, including the electronic arts, have a major role in educating students

In reality, few schools display all these markers. However, writing practices like blogging allow more schools to move toward using multiple intelligence theory in the curriculum. Like other multimedia formats, blogging introduces students to new creative outlets for their writing, artistic, spatial, and musical talents while fulfilling most states' technology requirements. And, blogging can be integrated through small, yet manageable curricular changes. Teachers who already use collaborative learning and computers in their classrooms can easily incorporate a blog for their students. For those teachers who are fairly inexpert or new to technology, blogging may require some training and rethinking about how to approach the writing process. However, the actual time it takes a teacher to accomplish these tasks and learn the blogging software is quite minimal.

At the very least, blogging can be a low-cost, effective localized method for encouraging individually tailored educational experiences that can reach most student populations. In schools where varied populations affect learning outcomes, students can maintain their dignity because the blogging process encourages each participant to contribute some knowledge or skill to maintain a blog. Given that most public school districts operate under policies of inclusion, the requirement that teachers incorporate writing tasks like blogging in their classrooms demonstrates that schools take seriously the notion of creating classroom practices that meet the needs of all students.

Such thinking is not Pollyannish. It is a goal that educators and parents should strive for to ensure that youngsters are ready for the challenges and demands technology brings in the future. Still, not every school district in America will embrace blogging as a classroom practice, just as not every district will embrace multiple intelligence theory as a way to counter the "skill, drill, and kill" model of the reborn movement in psychometric assessments of learning.

However, there are schools that do integrate blogging as well as multiple intelligence theory in the student learning process. Such schools can be exemplars of cultures where alternative assessments of student academic competency exist. A school culture in which youngsters learn by assimilating, transmitting, and transforming knowledge into new meaningful units seems to be the place where multiple intelligence theory and blogging work best.

These school cultures tend to nurture rather than undermine students' latent creativity and tacit knowledge. Such an atmosphere cultivates students' intellectual curiosity, interest, and wonderment about the world. Blogging activities can encourage higher-level thinking processes to take place because all students are working toward greater teacher expectations and understanding of class material.

Blogging can either supplement or replace traditional textbook teaching. For teachers, this can be a godsend. Blogging activities sometimes free classroom teachers from the bind of approaching material in a single-minded or set manner for twenty-five to forty students who are progressing at different cognitive and social paces. Because blogs give users the flexibility to enter into problem solving or discussions from multiple venues, students are able to find the route most appropriate for their learning styles or levels of competency once they access the material.

Moreover, as with any multimedia focus on learning, with blogs, students discover that there are many perspectives surrounding any historical, literary, scientific, mathematical, or cultural event. Most textbooks rarely present such diverse perspectives to students, which accounts for the simplicity many adolescents display in their thinking about complex issues. As professors and employers so often pronounce in the media, few graduating students develop the important deliberative and evaluative skills needed to manage complicated or voluminous information.

Blogs can become an important educational tool in changing that perception because students can engage with material that challenges their assumptions and participate in discussions in ways that complement their learning styles. As a result, they acquire the critical thinking skills needed to succeed later on in college or in the workplace.

For students who have difficulties mastering the core academic subjects, such as reading and writing, blogging can be a lifeline. Many times, these students are intelligent, but their abilities do not match up well with traditional school-based learning. Quite often, students who have competency problems in traditional learning environments also have difficulty in accessing the types of materials used in classrooms. Because of changes in a family's socioeconomic status, a lack of parental interest in education, or other conditions that can affect a student's ability to access print literature, these students are left behind.

Still, through a blog, students can demonstrate their understanding of classroom information. On blogs, students can construct maps, images, or photographs to illustrate their aesthetic intelligence or compose musical scores modeled after pieces from various periods to explore the historical significance of each style and to demonstrate their musical intelligence. Students can also use online materials from libraries, historical organizations, and other archives to demonstrate their academic knowledge beyond the usual logico-linguistic intelligence expected of students.

Blogs provide students with many ways to make learning meaningful. Thus, underperforming students have more options for becoming literate. However, teachers, parents, and administrators must not rely only on grades from blogging assignments to assess student progress.

Alternative assessment tools, such as electronic portfolios, a public blog, teachers' observational notes or teaching journal entries, open exhibitions of student work, individualized rubrics, and so on, need to be established before blogging can be integrated into any classroom. Alternative assessments can enhance relations between parents and educators because the community can see what students are learning and how they are mastering this information in various ways.

In many instances, schools and parents will need to see multiple sources of evaluation—for example, short teacher observation narratives about the class, an electronic portfolio, and SAT scores—to identify those students who are academically on target and those who need remediation. Several resources for evaluation potential offer a more solid foundation for assessing student achievement, certainly far more concrete than the current limited picture that state writing tests or SAT exams provide students and their parents.

Neither technology nor a theory of intelligence either alone or together can improve student learning without clearly defined educational goals. A supportive school culture and academic mission are important for shaping students' academic goals. These priorities must be made explicit to students, their parents, and the community so that all constituencies understand how and why blogs are being used in student learning.

USING MULTIPLE INTELLIGENCE THEORY AND BLOGGING TO CREATE TALENTED TEENS

Blending multiple intelligence theory with blogging provides an environment where youngsters can master required skills like writing, reading, and information processing and also enhance those talents that shape their individuality, such as artistic, musical, interpersonal, and intrapersonal strengths. A good number of today's high school students are disinterested, discouraged, and distracted in most classroom situations because of the way subject material is presented to them. Savvy educators know that motivating students to learn and reducing student drama are crucial for developing student talents.

Drawing upon multiple intelligence theory and blogging may be a way for educators to mix social and academic spheres of learning. Classes where teachers integrate multiple intelligence theory with blogging appear to pique students' interest in learning particular subjects. Students find that combining the social and academic spheres of learning while blogging helps them overcome onerous or challenging tasks. Mihaly Csikszentmihalyi (1997) observed that people who use their skills to the maximum degree possible "enjoy the hardships and challenges of their task." These individuals are able to turn seemingly meaningless or intimidating experiences into enjoyable ones.

For years, education theorists have emphasized that making learning a pleasurable experience is crucial for developing the talents of students. Activities that spur interest tend to motivate students toward scholastic achievement. Blogging taps into the basic desire of teenagers to communicate with others; this drive to socialize is a priority that nearly all teenagers have. Multiple intelligence theory gives educators a framework to help students discover the routes for communicating with blog readers. Students thus develop an interest in writing that rewards them in ways that the clear and rational models of traditional expository prose do not. And, as most writing specialists suggest, once students have a deep personal investment in the writing process, they will develop the verbal and mechanical fluency and organizational skills necessary to move forward.

Csikszentmihalyi (1997) notes that the two most undesirable conditions for student learning are anxiety and boredom. As Csikszentmihalyi explains, when schools or parents expect too much from their teens, anxiety emerges. Conversely, when schools or parents expect too little, boredom takes hold. Therefore, curricular expectations need to be on par with the abilities of students at each grade level so that their motivation to learn and their ability to achieve continue to increase.

Especially when combined with multiple intelligence theory, blogging activities are flexible enough that students with a range of abilities can develop their skills throughout the middle and high school years. In tandem, blogs and multiple intelligence theory would fit well into the spiral curriculum model that psychologist Jerome Bruner outlined in his 1960 book, *The Process of Education*.

According to Bruner, the complexity of the curriculum develops as the course plan continually revisits and builds upon basic ideas until students grasp the full formal apparatus that goes with the concepts. As students gain mastery of the subject's tools and system, the activities grow more complex to match student growth. For instance, students would learn how to create blogs and focus on the verbal, mechanical, organizational, and grammatical skills in the early stages of presenting content. Then, as students became more proficient with these basic ideas in writing, they would move into learning rhetorical strategies for addressing audiences through written and visual content.

Again, as students gain mastery in these rhetorical techniques, teachers layer in a small, manageable amount of material to study in greater depth, so students continually practice the range of skills and abilities they learned in previous lessons. Applying multiple intelligence theory to this approach suggests that students would learn to blog by harnessing their strongest intelligences. Over time, other intelligences would be developed as students work on their blogs and on their writing.

Quite a few teachers I work with who approach blogging through multiple intelligence theory find that far more students in their classes should be considered "talented," even though the standard measures of intelligence would indicate otherwise. Like me, these teachers have learned that the common cognitive tests used to label a student "talented" are somewhat suspect if all students are exposed to a learning environment that cultivates a range of academic, social, and cultural skills. It may be found that students' talents exceed a single test, or that talented teens might be found where educators and parents may least expect.

Human talent is made up of more than one high test score on a given day. Besides biological factors, emotional, personal, familial, cultural, and social factors also shape an individual's talent. How educators and parents come to understand better the ways to nurture adolescents' talents may lead to more effective options for teaching all students.

Many talented teenagers have difficulties in reaching their potential because they come from a family that lacks financial resources, social contacts, or familial cohesiveness. Consequently, it is important for educators to address these factors.

Regular blogging develops students' talents because it involves the organization of information, the motivation to write about this information, and the discipline to create a set of habits to concentrate on disseminating this information to a larger audience. As a structured educational activity, blogging can bring solid learning communities to talented teenagers from disadvantaged backgrounds. Blogging also allows them to tap into interests that are undiscovered, undervalued, or unnoticed in the school or home but that have an external audience. For students who already come from more advantaged backgrounds, blogging enriches or enhances the talents they already display. For those students who are new English language learners, blogging can assist them in acquiring the hands-on, colloquial usage needed to be a proficient user of a second language.

If educators and parents want to cultivate the talents of teenagers, then both parties must encourage students to blog in the context of multiple intelligence theory. Drawing upon the work of Csikszentmihalyi (1997) to describe the commonalities of adolescent talent, I present below four reasons that I feel best summarize the importance of classroom blogging mediated by multiple intelligence theory:

- Blogging encourages students to use various intelligences and provides intrinsic motivation and external recognition to learn.
- Blogging can compete with "learning diversions" like TV, popular culture, and commodity culture.
- Blogging can showcase talented students in ways that do not necessarily always make them "different" from their peers.
- Blogging through the use of multiple intelligence theory reduces a number of the obstacles that talented learners face in schools.

In the first instance, bloggers must use various intellectual abilities to generate a useful blog. Most teenage bloggers are motivated to build blog spaces that receive external praise from peers or visitors. The more visits and posts left on a blog, the greater the blogger's motivation to learn.

Educators and parents continually lament that schooling cannot compete with all the external cultural forces that impinge upon the classroom. Blogging competes favorably against other cultural media as a learning tool. Today's students are digital natives, and many have a degree of familiarity with blogging as a communication genre. Still, there is much a teacher can show students about blogging to enhance the experience as a learning tool.

One of the reasons teenage girls, like many other students, choose not to develop their academic or intellectual talents is because they would be perceived as different from others at a time in life when no one wants to be viewed as different. Encouraging students to tap into their dominant intelligences when creating a blog helps teens showcase their abilities without encountering social isolation. Talented student bloggers are often considered "cool" or "in demand" because of their intelligence in this area, a perception that can transfer to wider social acceptance in school. Such acceptance can make the process of school-ing more tolerable for talented students.

Last, schools are filled with obstacles to learning like standardized tests or tedious learning methods that do not necessarily reflect a stu-dent's talent. Blogging provides an outlet where students can demon-strate their multiple intelligences in a public venue. As a structured learning activity, blogging can give teachers, administrators, and parents an idea of how well students have internalized lessons. Because blogs are normally produced for external audiences, the student work on a blog can confirm or corroborate the learning at school that can't be mea-sured on a single test.

A well-developed student blog gives a complex picture of how stu-dents learn portable writing and thinking skills. Highly qualified teach-ers can discover that balance between showing students how to practice basic skills that can be applied in multiple contexts while encouraging students to explore their intellectual freedom and sensitivity to new ma-terial. To challenge and encourage deeper, critical thinking in their stu-dents, educators need to make blogs a quality activity that enriches and makes learning pleasurable throughout the middle and high school years.

IS THERE A BLOG IN THIS CLASS?

Stefanie Fox, Olga Polites, and Melissa Brinkmann are secondary lan-guage arts/English teachers from southern New Jersey who regularly use blogs in their classrooms. While each teacher employs her blog dif-ferently based on the students' grade level, each teacher recognizes that blogs represent writing and reading that have "different demands, dif-ferent forms of imagination" (Kress & van Leeuwen, 2003). (Stefanie Fox and Melissa Brinkmann have graciously given me permission to ref-erence their blogs for interested educators and parents. To visit Stefanie's blog, set the browser to www.literaturedragon.blogspot.com. To visit Melissa's personal blog, set the browser to brinkdogsblog.blogspot.com. Melissa Brinkmann uses Nicenet.org's private blogging space to work with her students, and to respect their privacy, that address has not been made public.)

In each of these classrooms, blogs extend the conversations that began earlier in the day or the week. Frequently, the students' writing is playful; sometimes the writing reflects a complex form of iconic writing symbolized by various keyboard strokes or alphabetic combinations. Certainly the students' manner of writing is less formal than one would expect to see in classroom settings.

Such writing mirrors the axiom, the mode affects the shaping of knowledge and its relation to power. The students' blog postings are not written in standard English in accordance with canonical knowledge gleaned from their textbooks. If viewers were to drop in unannounced to these class blogs, they would see students who are reading and interpreting information based on their experiences and how those incidents shape their tacit, cultural, and school-based knowledge. Students writing on these blogs are attending to the "now" of learning—what they need to know for the present and near future as well as what they need to know for a specific purpose.

As Guenther Kress observes (Kress & van Leeuwen, 2003), learning in this manner is not how most adults became literate. Many educators and parents were taught to read and write through continual rigorous attention directed toward a particular text. In the past, we might have called this type of literacy instruction "long-view thinking" (Graves, 2003). Learning to read and write required reflection, deliberation, and problem solving. Such are the foundations for logico-linguistic intelligence (Gardner 1993, 1999).

Blogging requires educators and parents to leave these notions of literacy behind to consider what it is becoming. It may be that in a society driven by information and information overload, students have to learn in a more directed fashion because there is far more data coming from multiple sources to process. When adults read teenagers' blogs, they see multiple intelligences at work, usually in tandem with other skills and abilities. It is as if the blogs are showing educators, parents, and the students a glimpse into a future educational agenda that is based on rapid intake and transmission of information that students filter with their varied competencies.

Stefanie, Olga, and Melissa believe in the power of blogging to reach their students. As teachers, they sense that blogs can be a great teaching tool to help students recapture aspects of the written word and take control of their learning. All three instructors note that blogging also changes the classroom dynamic because of the subtle power shift on the blogs. Melissa made this point about how the classroom dynamic changes when students blog:

> The students enter class after a night of blogging with all kinds of things they want to say to each other and to me. First of all, Nicenet makes them want to do their homework, and when I make responses mandatory, even the students who don't speak up in class will post some pretty deep and honest remarks and thoughts. Blogging has brought us closer and it even connects different class periods. One honors class talks to the other via Nicenet, etc. I am also able to respond individually to students' remarks, which is difficult to do in a forty-two-minute period with over thirty students. What a thrill! (personal correspondence, June 6, 2006)

Melissa is not the only teacher satisfied with the students' blogging experiences in class. In a course paper about integrating blogging into the language arts classroom, Stefanie notes,

> Blogs prove to be promising for the classroom experience. I get to communicate with my students beyond the classroom after they have had time to think about topics and discussions in class. Being able to connect with my students in another type of community is what I love and appreciate most about the blogging experience. The students and I get to know one another better—fostering the learning that takes place in my classroom. We have a community where people can interact comfortably. The blog helps students understand and clarify difficult assignments. Blogging can be used for modeling and scaffolding—two important terms in learning theory. More importantly, blogging gets my students constructing thoughts and interacting with others through writing. (Fox, 2006)

I agree with several of Stefanie's comments: Students are frequently more comfortable writing in blog-based environments, which makes it crucial for teachers to be aware of coded or acronymic language, "leet speak" or its equivalent. ("Leet" or "1337" speak is a type of creole or pidgin language that emerged from Bulletin Board Systems in the early stages of the Internet. Leet speak was adapted to the Internet Relay Chat (IRC) and Instant Messenger (IM), and now leet speak is common with teenagers on blogs, IM, or with other online discourse. A simple Google search for "leet speak" will provide educators and parents with several reputable sites that can help adults break the lexical, syntactic, and semantic codes.) Two of the greatest problems that exist for the teaching of writing are that students are not always cognizant of either their audiences or purposes in composing. As a result, many teenagers forget to switch their codes from leet speak to standard English. This is a point Stefanie also addresses:

> I know my students blog all of the time; however, I was fearful that because this blog was school-related, they would not participate. I was also concerned that if the students did participate, would they keep on the topic of the post and not drift into inappropriate topics? Furthermore, would the students use their real names when posting, so I would know who they are? Also, how would I deal with inappropriate commenting?
>
> I was thrilled to see that a few people posted right away and that the content of all posts was acceptable. However, what I feared was already happening: the first post came from a <33. Although what this person posted was wonderful, I still wanted to know the writer of the comments.
>
> Addressing display names was the first issue I focused on with maintaining this blog. The other main issue with maintaining this blog is getting more students to participate in blogging about literature. I have the same group of students participating all of the time. (Fox, 2006)

On a typical assignment, students' failure to switch their linguistic codes may lower their grade a bit. Difficulties with linguistic code switching often occur when students write traditional papers that shift between home language and school discourse. This is a common situation most students face at some point in their schooling.

However, on standardized or state-mandated writing tests, where the stakes are high for schools and students, such absentmindedness can be devastating. Schools and students are penalized for these discursive slip-ups. As Stefanie's comments illustrate, teachers will have to discuss appropriate use of school-based blogging so students have the correct frame from which to participate. How teachers decide to address these concerns will vary from instructor to instructor.

Melissa acknowledges discourse issues on her class blog in the following comment:

When I sign onto the blog during class to rehash or highlight what's being discussed, I often read aloud what has been written and emphasize the acronyms, abbreviations, misspellings, etc. so that students are aware of the differences between blogging, speaking, and formal writing. It is fun to try to speak the way that students blog and, through humor, students begin to notice the different modes of language that they use to communicate with each other. (personal correspondence, June 6, 2006)

Stefanie, Olga, and Melissa tackle these issues by talking through linguistic code switching issues with their students. Some writing tasks, like blogging, encourage creativity in language use. Other writing situations, such as those on mandated tests, require standard language forms. Teacher guidance on this issue helps students use their competencies in appropriate ways.

From studying how Stefanie, Olga, and Melissa address language and discourse concerns through blogging in their classrooms, I have seen how teachers can facilitate reading and writing practices using blogs. Let me address three clear areas where I see these teachers' blogs addressing significant literacy concerns:

- Blogging may encourage students to read and write more.
- Blogs may be a source of pleasure for students.
- Blogs may ensure that reading and writing for pleasure continue past students' college years.

Embracing the influence of pleasure in blogging is crucial for encouraging literacy skills. Students who see writing and reading as primarily school-based activities tend to become aliterate—they can read, but they do not wish to read outside of required academic situations. Getting some aliterate students to welcome blogging into their daily practices is a step toward using literacy as an enrichment activity that can build student vocabulary, syntax, and fluency. Moreover, if aliterate students come to find that writing and reading can be pleasurable activities, blogging could be a bridge between academic and leisure reading.

Once students find pleasure in blogging, they will continue to blog long after they complete their course of study. Because blogging is conducted in shorter spurts (as opposed to leisure reading or journal writing, which is thought to take too much of students' time), it takes little to no time to post a blog entry. The brevity of most blog posts is a draw for many aliterates. The allure of reading short, direct posts rather than long, flowing pages appeals to those who are not strong readers. Similarly, writing a short post rather than a lengthy essay can be very attractive for resistant or uncomfortable writers.

With publication assured, bloggers always have an opportunity to create a genuine readership for their ideas. These two elements take away the school-based feeling people frequently associate with writing. If one writes or reads for pleasure, then the type of gatekeeping found in school is an unnecessary feature.

Stefanie, Olga, and Melissa all have a blog in their classes, as do hundreds of other elementary and secondary school classes around the country. These three instructors would probably be the first to admit that blogs have a "more-more" relationship with literacy—the more reading and writing that students do, the more literate they become.

Teachers who maintain classroom blogs as an educational tool offer students added advantages in their literacy. In class, students are exposed to lots of reading and writing, and then they extend those same experiences to blogging. As Griswold, McDonnell, and Wright (2005) observed, in these situations, the advantages come from several distinct areas:

- Information possession from varied sources
- Social connections made in and out of classes
- Cultural capital and the ability to find contacts under new conditions
- Adaptation to new circumstances in learning

Reclaiming blogging for educational purposes is crucial if educators and parents hope to ensure that teenagers have the skills, competencies, intelligences, and abilities needed for literacy in the years ahead. The Internet is not going away. Over time, blogs will be replaced by new communication modes, and today's students will need to be able to adapt to these newer forms. Teachers like Stefanie Fox, Olga Polites, and Melissa Brinkmann are leading the way for their students to gain a double advantage in their current and future learning experiences. The blogs in these teachers' classes tap into students' multiple intelligences without sacrificing standards, state mandated literacy skills, or community expectations.

The question is, why aren't more schools (and teachers) following their lead?

CREATING CLASSROOM
ETHICS FOR BLOGGING

Educators and parents can prevent some of the problems with teenage blogging. Rather than installing firewalls that bar students from generating blogs or setting up "sting operations" to ferret out inappropriate student content—both of which undermine student trust in schools, parents, and local institutions—a more prudent solution may be to create a code of ethics for blogging. Drawing upon standards from the school, community, and students to design a code of blogging ethics teaches students about civic participation and integrates community standards into the learning experience.

Just as most schools set codes of ethics for other student behaviors, they must also provide ethical guidelines for blogging. As I noted in earlier chapters, the problems that arise in schools when adolescents are blogging, like bullying or relational aggressiveness, represent larger issues that spill over from schools to other environments. Ethical codes provide a model for students to establish a mutually beneficial, pleasant, and productive learning environment. When all members affected in a school community—parents and community members as well as students, teachers, and administrators—form these ethical codes for blogging, all parties are more likely to view the guidelines as a voluntary set of practices for governing cooperative behaviors rather than mandatory rules.

A measure for instituting a code of ethics for blogging could be a fresh way to address civic responsibility in the student body and in the community at large. Such a measure would cover six crucial areas that are now left open to wide-ranging, after-the-fact speculation:

- Define acceptable and appropriate student behaviors for blogging
- Promote a high set of expectations for student practices in writing, communicating, and socializing with others
- Provide a benchmark for measuring student proficiency in developing online materials or technology expertise
- Establish a framework for maintaining responsible community behaviors
- Proffer reasonable standards of online conduct in relation to the school's mission
- Offer students a description of the educational purposes of blogging

Of course, a code of ethics cannot prevent problems with or breaches of student conduct, but it can provide a system for handling concerns as they arise. Moreover, with an ethical code designed and agreed upon by the schools, parents, and students, concerns related to blogging are more likely to be reduced because all members have had a say in its design and enforcement.

WRITING A CODE OF ETHICS

A code of ethics within an educational setting highlights the values, the sensitivities, and the judgments shared by a group of individuals. Generating an ethical code requires the planners to engage in several steps. Here is a list of potential items to address in designing a code of ethics:

- What is the purpose of this ethical code? To inspire positive community behaviors? To regulate student behavior? To curb infractions?
- Is the ethical code designed to mete out punishment or to guide students' behaviors when they blog?
- Is there an aspirational section to the ethical code; that is, does the code have a section where there are communal ideals and expectations students are to live up to? Are there sets of values and principles listed that the school, the community, and the students should maintain when blogging?

- Is there a section on enforcing various infractions?
- How will this code of ethics be reviewed, enforced, and revised, and how often?
- Who will create, maintain, and revise this code of ethics?

Certainly other items can be addressed in a code for ethical blogging depending on local school district needs and concerns. This list only addresses core issues found in most codes of ethics and can be tailored to fit specific student or community needs. Those generating an ethical code for blogging must address three significant areas:

- Increasing bloggers' ethical sensitivity and judgment in posting comments
- Developing bloggers' moral courage and agency to act in socially responsible ways or to handle conflicting or compromising online situations
- Defining morally permissible boundaries for expressing ideas in language

Ethical codes for blogging in the schools will look as different as the groups that engage in the creation process. Certainly, the expectations and values for elementary grade students will differ from those for the middle school or high school grades. Likewise, public and private schools may have ethical codes for blogging that reflect the specific missions of the schools and the populations they serve.

To ensure that the ethical code for blogging is considered fair and equitable in the community, a group consisting of parents, teachers, students, administrators, key community leaders, and the school board should form to plan and write the document. Ideally, in order for the planning and writing process to move quickly, no more than ten individuals should be selected to form this working group; however, the group must strive to have a representative voice from each population affected. Students, for instance, need to be involved in the planning and writing of this code, as they will be the ones most likely to have the greatest stake in the process. Community members, such as law enforcement or mental health professionals, may want to serve to ensure local standards are preserved.

Many times, the public views ethical codes as mere "window dress-ing": codes that are designed with good intentions but that are meaning-less. For an ethical code to be effective in a school setting, it has to reflect the school's essential values and virtues. Sometimes this means community members' positions need to be modified to echo the school's purpose or mission. Who would be best suited to serve on a committee drafting an ethical code for blogging? The following five questions pro-vide a starting point for those who must select committee members:

1. What populations are most affected by this code of ethics, and what is their priority in the school's mission?
2. What is the main action the school wants to take with this ethical code in relation to blogging?
3. What unethical decisions related to blogging does the school wish to prevent, and how can these situations be prevented?
4. What types of ethical situations have arisen related to blogging in the school or what types of ethical situations are expected?
5. What are the steps for handling conflicting principles or similar ethical breaches in the school?

Once the drafting committee is set, the real work of planning and writ-ing the code of ethics begins. Depending on the committee's focus, the ethical code may be brief or lengthy; it may be designed with principles and guidelines in mind or be more relationship-based. The finished product may be sentences, paragraphs, or pages. However, at its core, an ethical code for blogging has to express a specific set of standards as well as provide concrete guidance on how everyone in the school can meet those standards. The language has to be understood by everyone affected by the document, from students and their parents to teachers and school administrators.

The idea in preparing an ethical code for blogging is to teach students the concept of "balance" in their writing and social behaviors, particu-larly when conflicting principles or situations arise. Blogging can be used in a variety of different situations, some school-based and some home-based. Here is where conflicting principles will arise. While stu-dents have the right to their own language outside of school, they do have to realize that some effects of language usage (and some discourse situations or contexts) outside of school carry over into the school building. In those situations, students have to learn to balance their choice of words with the potential effects. Well-planned ethical codes for blogging should address the actions a school may take if out-of-school blogging issues enter the classroom. As a result, it may take the committee longer to draft these sections of an ethical code and to ensure that fairness and legal issues are addressed before publishing the document.

In this process, there is one caveat: regardless of how optimistically or how carefully the committee plans and implements an ethical code for blogging, members should be aware that criticism will come from some quarters. Many times, the criticism is well placed: the ethical code is too brief or sketchy to guide students and teachers in defining appropriate behaviors. Conversely, some will argue that the ethical code is too draconian or punitive. In either instance, the ethical code needs to be revised so students and teachers can adhere to the guidelines and the principles seem equitable for all.

Some criticisms can be handled proactively through selecting quality committee members. Those who are knowledgeable about blogging, about students, and about the community at large make good participants. Also important is that the committee members have no ideological, political, or other agenda in the community, since they may become targets of criticism levied by those who bear grudges against them. Lastly, whenever possible, the committee should ensure that the decision making process is as transparent as possible once a draft of the code of ethics has been presented to the public.

Transparency in this sense means the committee shares the document at open school board sessions, elicits feedback from parent-school organizations, discusses the guidelines with student council or other student leadership groups, and offers key community figures a chance to read and comment on the material. Feedback from all these constituencies ensures that everyone connected to the school has a chance to respond and to take ownership in making sure the guidelines are followed.

THREE MODEL ETHICAL CODES

Using the heuristic information presented in this chapter, I provide three model ethics codes in this section that schools and parents can adapt to address blogging in school or classroom situations. The language and the content of any ethics code or policy document should be vetted by legal and local authorities before the school implements the policies. These examples are offered only as illustrations of the type of information found in ethical codes for students and faculty.

Model I: A Guidelines-Based Approach

The following is the Smith School's Code of Ethics and Values for Blogging and Internet Use: Smith School's Code of Ethics and Values for Blogging and Internet Use reflects the broad beliefs our school has for the community. Written in spring 2006 by a committee of ten individuals, drawn from students, teachers, administrators, and board members as well as key local township members, the Smith School's Code of Ethics and Values was modified in August 2006 by the Smith School District's attorney and the full Board of Education. What is presented in the paragraphs that follow has been approved by students, teachers, school administrators, parents, community members, and the board of trustees.

Preamble

The Smith School's Code of Ethics and Values for Blogging and Internet Use provides clear, positive statements for student, teacher, and administrator use of blogs, personal web spaces, and other Internet use on school grounds. Our Code of Ethics and Values presents practical strategies for classroom use of blogging, web spaces, or other Internet capabilities and offers a framework for handling day-to-day situations that surround blogging, personal web spaces, or other Internet use on school grounds.

Goals of Smith School's Code of Ethics and Values for Blogging

Our hope is to make Smith School a better community by ensuring blogging, personal web spaces, and Internet use on the school grounds

- Is grounded in the mutual respect of students, teachers, staff, and administrators

- Is designed on a system of trust between students and their peers, students and their teachers or staff, and students and school administration
- Is intended to promote only the highest standards of excellence in personal and professional conduct of all school members

Smith School's Three Values of Ethical Blogging and Internet Use

1. As a member of the Smith School community, my blogs, web pages, or other Internet use will be ethical. In practice, ethical behavior looks like the following:

   - Writing to reflect integrity and good judgment
   - Uploading content that is honest, truthful, and does not harm another Smith School student, teacher, staff member, or administrator
   - Having a web or blog presence that shows respect for others in the community

2. As a member of the Smith School community, my blogs, web pages, or other Internet use will be collaborative. In practice, collaborative behavior looks like the following:

   - Acting cooperatively with others in a tolerant and understanding manner
   - Treating diverse opinions or ideas with an open mind
   - Accomplishing individual goals or tasks in a timely manner to help other group members meet their goals and tasks

3. As a member of the Smith School community, my blogs, web pages, or other Internet use will be responsible. In practice, responsible behavior looks like the following:

   - Avoiding inflammatory or derogatory language
   - Displaying content that is not sexually provocative
   - Not giving out personal contact information or school location

Smith School's Penalties for Breaking the Code of Ethics for Blogging

Students who are found to violate the Smith School's Code of Ethics for Blogging and Internet Use are subject to the following penalties:

First offense. No access to the Media Center for one week. Parental notification.

Second offense. No access to the Media Center for a marking period. Parental notification. Detention or in-school suspension, depending on severity of infraction.

Third offense. No access to the Media Center for entire school year. Parental notification. Detention or in-school suspension, depending on severity of infraction. Student/parent/school official conference required.

When implemented, the guidelines-based approach clearly outlines acceptable behaviors and punishments that students, teachers, staff, and administrators can understand. Because of the possibility that some ethical code violations can introduce outside influences that affect students' lives, it is important to have parental notification for infractions. Parents need to be made aware that their children—or other children—may be playing on the Internet in unhealthy, perhaps even dangerous, ways.

However, some schools may not feel the need to construct a guidelines-based code of ethics for student blogging or Internet use. In these situations, a second model may be more appropriate. Student pledges, similar to an honor code, are written by student leaders in conjunction with faculty and administration.

There is a social implication that occurs when students agree to and sign an ethical code they create, even if some students may break the code. For older students, for private schools with concrete missions, or for schools that already function using the honor system, the second model presented below may be more effective.

Model 2: The Student Pledge Approach

The following is the Smith School Code of Ethics for the Blogging Student Pledge:

Smith School students promote the ethical, respectful, and fair use of blogs, personal web pages, or other Internet communication systems on school grounds. The Smith School community agrees that socially respon-sible use of technology is important in today's society. All members of the Smith School believe everyone shares in making sure computer technol-ogy benefits the community. Therefore, all students, teachers, staff, and administrators will use their blogs, personal web pages, or other Internet communication systems in respectful, honest, and tolerant ways. We will not bully, attack Smith School students, teachers, staff, or administrators, or use computer technology to cheat on papers or tests.

The pledge model differs from a guideline-based model in that usually everyone in the school community is given a card to sign and carry as evidence that they agree to the policy. Most schools connect the pledge for ethical blogging to their larger honor code or ethics policy.

Some schools have specific penalties listed for violations of the honor code or pledge, which can include expulsion. Any punishment for breaking the pledge or honor code needs to be addressed by all school groups, from students to school attorneys, before the pledge is agreed upon in the school.

Model 3: The Mission Statement Approach

The following is the Smith School Code of Ethics for Blogging and Internet Use:

Smith School, the public middle school in Smithville, NJ, is part of the Smithville Unified School District in Warren County. Smith School stu-dents, teachers, staff, and administration believe that responsible use of the Internet, including blogging and personal web pages, is an important part of literacy and learning in the 21st century. We agree that responsible use of blogs, personal web pages, e-mail, podcasts, or other Internet com-munication systems includes being respectful of Smith School and Smith-ville members, tolerant of diverse opinions, and knowledgeable about disseminating personal information online. Therefore, Smith School stu-dents, teachers, staff, and administrators will use blogs, personal web pages, e-mail, podcasts, or other Internet communication systems to strive for excellence in information literacy and in education and not to harm, harass, or intimidate others.

As with the student pledge, the mission statement approach is a broad-based policy that outlines the general vision and philosophy for a school or a classroom. A mission statement tends to address a goal to reach rather than a set of guidelines to put into action.

Mission statement models are frequently the target of criticism because most are broadly written and hard to enforce. However, given the political climate of some districts, a mission statement model may be the only possible option for introducing a code for ethical blogging into a district or a school.

School and student leaders know their communities best. When a committee drafts its code of ethics for blogging and Internet use, constant revision and sharing should be integral parts of the process. Whether the result is a code that is more directive—like the guideline approach—or more relational—like the student pledge or mission statement—what matters is that schools forge a policy that all stakeholders, from students and their parents to teachers and administrators, can agree upon.

DOING WHAT EDUCATORS DO BEST

Educators are at their best when they are teaching others. When a code of ethics for blogging works well, it outlines visible actions for behaviors and is consistent with federal, state, and local learning standards or policies. In addition, the ethical code outlines how the school relates to the external community in the expectations that the school has for students. When students become involved in the process of writing a code of ethics for their behavior, they learn about civics, politics, and social action firsthand.

After constant practice in writing and sharing this process, schools will be able to generate ethical codes like the one proposed here for blogging that instill public confidence in them and lead to greater trust. An ethical code for blogging needs to complement local standards and practices, not create substitutes for those areas. As the public learns about the school district, so too do school administrators learn about the community. This is especially true if dramatic changes in population or rapid industrial growth or decline have altered the area in recent years.

Because blogging is a dynamic process, once the ethical code is established, it must be revisited periodically. Simply writing, printing, posting, and announcing this code of ethics will not be enough. A standing committee needs to oversee changes in technological advances and their implications for the ethical code. This committee evaluates the existing ethical code for blogging, identifies alternatives whenever advances occur in software or hardware technologies that shape blogging, and recommends changes in the ethical code when appropriate. Whether the schools decide this committee meets regularly or on an ad hoc basis depends upon the institution's organizational flow, but there should be a standing committee available to review the code and recommend changes.

Blogging, like all other online communication, should be a learning experience. Educators are at their best when they take the lead and show their communities how learning takes place. In the 21st century, an increasing amount of learning occurs online—whether on a blog, with a podcast, or on a web page. Ethical codes related to student use of electronic media give parents and community members a sense of trust that their schools recognize the importance this type of learning has in students' lives. Moreover, when students, parents, and community members have the opportunity to contribute to the creation of ethical codes, they can see that the school values their input as well as their cooperation in shaping the community. In this way, ethical codes for blogging or other Internet use provide educators with an opportunity to engage the community in a large-scale civics lesson that bears a direct influence on the classroom. This is, of course, what educators do best: They teach not only the word but the world.

⑩

BLOGGING MATTERS

This last chapter answers my original question: Why blog? Because blogging matters.

This book has been an attempt to explain why blogging is an important new approach for teaching and learning and not just another silly teenage activity. Right now, blogging is on the verge of being dismissed as a superficial activity. That is a shame, as blogging simultaneously teaches students how to master language use, writing, critical thinking, and multimedia use. Blogging is an important genre for education at all levels and with all student populations, a genre too important for educators and parents to ignore.

From my perspective, blogs have created a new portal for student learning in online environments. Teachers, administrators, and parents who deny blog access to students may be doing more harm than good. While mainstream media reports portray blogs and personal websites as prurient or superficial or both, savvy tech users know that these electronic genres hold great promise for student learning. As I have tried to argue throughout this book, part of being literate in the 21st century includes the ability to write in online environments. Compared to other forms of literacy, online literacy places different demands on students' cognitive and social practices.

Unlike traditional reading and writing methods or processes, blogging requires students to be active learners. Active learning means students shape the information they take in and make that material their own. Whether they are acquiring mathematical, scientific, historical, or other content knowledge online, students have to develop more sophisticated literacy skills to differentiate unnecessary material and useful material. Then, to communicate that knowledge to others, students must hone their writing skills—not just mechanical or grammatical ability, but presentation and rhetorical facility—for a broad audience. Beyond these concrete skills, students must also know how to select the best medium for transmitting their knowledge. In an increasingly global, technologically-based society, that means students need to have proficiency in multimedia use and evaluation. Through blogging, students begin that process of developing multimedia competencies.

Currently, in higher education, blogs are being replaced with wikis, podcasts, and audioblogs as faculty strive to meet the demands of students for 24/7 learning experiences and the expectations of accrediting agencies and employers for increased information literacy. Blogs and other similar tools allow students the opportunity for asynchronous, on-demand learning that helps students develop at their own pace. The multimedia capabilities of blogs, wikis, podcasts, and audioblogs also allow students to use varied intelligences, a process that reinforces learning and the retention of complex course material. Consequently, blogs and their variants are differentiated learning tools par excellence.

Because K–12 or K–13 schools prepare students to enter colleges and universities, teachers and administrators have to be aware of what students will face as they move into advanced learning experiences. Parents too have to understand that information literacy and technological proficiency are becoming a crucial component of post-secondary education. This is especially true as colleges and universities attempt to educate students for a global working environment where large numbers of jobs will be in occupations that do not currently exist or ones that are being transformed through technology. As most professors and employers will attest, asynchronous learning environments, just like asynchronous workplaces, are commonplace in higher education. For K–12 or K–13 students to be well educated in the 21st century, information literacy and asynchronous access to course content are as important as standard literacy practices and good character. Consequently, blogging is more than a "kid's game" or a diary for teenagers to express their angst. When used properly in academic settings, even in the elementary grades, blogging can be an important asynchronous learning tool.

In asynchronous learning environments, students can adapt course materials to their intellectual strengths. Through multimedia presentations on blogs, students can tap into various experiences that enhance their learning. Writing and thinking, for instance, become a collaborative venture without the housekeeping distractions that frequently plague a traditional classroom, such as announcements, off-the-topic questions, unruly students, and attendance problems. Rather than enduring ineffective downtime during these classroom maintenance moments, teachers can place students in cooperative arrangement around computer stations. Valuable learning often takes place when students work together to solve a problem, pose questions, or challenge course content.

All of these factors are important not only for students with learning challenges or language or motivational difficulties but also for students who want to move at a faster pace than the others in a class. With either student population, a blog can minimize the chances that students will drop out of classes or school from frustration or boredom related to the class pacing. Of course, any effective asynchronous learning environment requires teachers to find their comfort zone with technology in the classroom. Depending on how a teacher segments a blog, enrichment assignments can be scheduled adjacent to remedial ones. That way, students can hone skill sets and advance to new applications once they feel they have mastered the basics. Peers can mentor or tutor another classmate in areas of the course work where they excel, even if they are weak in another area of the course. As an asynchronous learning tool, blogs transform the focus of classrooms from teachers to students.

Still, I do not want to paint a completely rosy picture of blogging in educational settings. There are problems. Yes, blogs and their counterparts produce highly student-centered classrooms and improve children's information literacy skills. Certainly, blogs are easy to set up and maintain, even for the most technophobic teacher. And I wholeheartedly agree that blogging in schools is a way to reach reticent learners, resistant students, and large numbers of learning-challenged students. However, there are five issues connected to blogging that teachers, parents, and administrators need to be aware of if school districts choose to implement this form of asynchronous learning.

FIVE CHALLENGES FACING CLASSROOM BLOGGING

I have been teaching with blogs for the past five years. Whether in undergraduate or graduate writing classes, in-service workshops for new or veteran teachers, or in seminars for college colleagues, the problems are similar. The first problem is that a blog is only as good or as useful as the blogger who builds it. This axiom is true regardless of where the blog exists in cyberspace.

The second problem relates to the first: Few teachers are blogging. They either see no educational reason to blog, have no desire to blog or to learn how to blog, or think blogging is some sort of kids' game. If teachers incorporate blogging into the curriculum without blogging themselves, as some do, then the blog is a miserable add-on. This axiom also holds true for school districts, grade levels, and college communities.

The first problem can be corrected with guidance and planning. The second problem is systemic in education. Both have to be addressed if students are to gain the technological literacies they need for future success. This section focuses on the issues that educators face when incorporating blogs in their classrooms.

For the most part, I see five challenges teachers face when they integrate blogging or any asynchronous learning activity into traditional classrooms. Because this book is primarily for K–12 or K–13 teachers, school administrators, and parents, I want to address these challenges specifically for the elementary, middle, and secondary school audience. However, college professors or instructors who read this book may find elements of their own teaching in what I outline below.

Challenge 1: Obtaining Adequate Training for Educators

The first challenge with blogging in K–12 or K–13 environments is ensuring that teachers and staff members have adequate training in blogging. Adequate training means more than a two-hour workshop after school showing faculty and staff how to blog. Teaching someone how to program blog software usually takes no more than thirty minutes. The learning curve for blogging is not steep. The real trick to implementing blogging in the classroom is for administrators to demonstrate how genuine learning relates to technology and to show teachers how to maintain a blog. Teaching someone how to integrate pedagogy with blog software takes time, experimentation, and the willingness to embrace ambiguity and error in the early stages. Maintaining a blog requires teachers to see the benefits of teaching through the blogosphere. With guidance and regular support, teachers can design incredibly effective blogs for asynchronous learning.

Assisting teachers in successfully integrating blogging across the curriculum means more than merely showing faculty how to set up a blog. It also means mentoring pedagogical change. Blogging complements the skilled teacher's repertoire: a teacher's imagination and expertise in both the subject and student development. But such innovation requires time to take hold in a curriculum. Teachers need time to design, replace, implement, and evaluate older instructional methods.

Rather than initiating sweeping wholesale changes in the curriculum to adapt to blogging, it may be more effective for administrators to ease two or three teachers per grade level into the process each year. Through a team-teaching approach, these individuals can adapt their teaching styles and methods to asynchronous learning through blogging. Then, borrowing from the "train-the-trainer" model, these teachers can teach several more teachers the following year until all teachers become familiar with integrating technology with pedagogy.

The gradual buy-in of teachers allows instructors to move into this new realm at their own pace. There will be early adopters or eager users who want to be the first to incorporate asynchronous learning tools into their courses. There will be some interested but technologically wary teachers. There will also be skeptics. School leaders need to tread carefully, as forcing all teachers to enter this discussion at the same time and at the same pace creates unnecessary conflict, which can subvert the administration's goals and affect student learning and attitudes toward blogging in the classroom.

If school administrators can plan to use asynchronous learning techniques over a period of two or three years, teachers will be able to see day by day how the techniques are transforming learning. Early adopters can lead the way and continue exploring new avenues while taking a leadership role with faculty, students, and parents. Early adopters can be the guides who lead others into the revised curriculum. They can also be valuable as trainers, because they understand the time, effort, and challenges others will face in adopting the new teaching tools.

Under this plan, interested but technologically unskilled teachers will have time to prepare themselves to move into this new classroom role. More skeptical teachers can ease themselves into the process as they see evidence that real learning—not gimmicks—is taking place. As technologies transform and the curriculum evolves to meet these demands, the early adopters and followers can continue to revise the curriculum to accommodate these changes.

But the curriculum is not the only area where teachers and staff need to become more proficient with blogging technologies. On-site workshops need to address the social dimensions of electronic communication such as how blogs, wikis, podcasts, or future electronic genres can help students define and transmit shifting identities and build social support systems in the classroom.

Challenge 2: Assessing Students' Blogs

A second challenge that teachers face when they want to incorporate blogs into the K–12 or K–13 classroom is assessment. As many have outlined elsewhere (Henderson, 2001; Penrod, 2005; Syverson, 2000; Whithaus, 2005), traditional classroom or writing assessment techniques have to be adapted to the learning that takes place in asynchronous environments. Standard rubrics on state assessment tests or in textbooks about essays are usually not appropriate for asynchronous media. Teachers will need time to develop suitable assessment tools for blogs, wikis, podcasts, or other future Internet-based genres for each grade level.

Classroom assessment techniques for blogs are different from techniques for paper texts because assessment is ongoing, rather than summative. Frequently, because blogging students are at various stages in their learning, feedback may have to take the form of specifically worded questions rather than a checklist. Short-answer responses that elicit teacher commentary seem to be the most helpful in developing student work. However, the change in an assessment rubric also alters the time it takes teachers to develop quality responses, and instructors must plan to conduct formative assessment if they decide to move into blogging.

For useful formative assessment, teacher responses should be fairly immediate and should provide both information and acknowledgment in the feedback. Information feedback is related to evaluation, grading, or commentary related to student content and production. Acknowledgment feedback is in the form of responses that recognize students have sent a post and signify that the teacher will respond soon, either privately or to the group. The two response modes are crucial for student progress, as one form shapes cognitive growth and the other, affective development.

Because some students access blogs from multiple locations—either at home, at school, or at a public venue—learning environments can look different. This factor can shape a finished product and the resulting assessment. Teachers cannot be sure where students access a blog; it may be in a noisy apartment, a student's bedroom, a school media center, or a local coffee shop. Locations can affect the responses of students or their attention spans in asynchronous learning, and this issue might have to be discussed with students who underperform or who perform beyond the abilities of other classmates on a regular basis.

To ensure students are doing their own work, some teachers might want to establish a classroom code of ethics—an honor code—in which students agree to be the ones who police themselves and their online behaviors. As I said earlier in the book, classroom ethical or honor codes serve as a way for students to learn moral agency related to their online activities so that they take more responsibility for their own learning.

Challenge 3: Creating Assignments That Matter

A third challenge to asynchronous teaching with blogs is that instruction depends upon a teacher's ability to construct well-designed assignments and tasks. Unlike the open classroom discussion format in a traditional classroom, blog exchanges need to be highly focused on a specific issue. In addition, students need to understand that evaluation occurs based on the quality of postings, not on the quantity posted. That is why teachers need to set clear expectations for the types of responses they hope to receive on blogs; otherwise, the group posts tend to be shallow, off the topic, or inane.

In the early stages of blogging in a classroom context, teachers need to lead students through the types of conversations that are appropriate for blogs used in academics. Students may want the right to use their own language and their own acronyms. While some colloquial language and acronymic usage might lend color, voice, and flavor to student postings, teachers have to ensure that these linguistic choices are correct for classroom situations. Many teachers who use blogs in their classrooms find that this issue is an excellent illustration of a writer's decisions regarding audience and purpose.

Similarly, successful blog-based courses, like any flourishing asynchronous course, have fixed deadlines for student submissions. This may come as a surprise to students who use blogs as a teenage communication tool, but virtually all research connected to asynchronous learning showed that even highly self-directed student learning contexts had fixed deadline dates for assignments. Students could work at their own paces as long as these dates were met.

In some ways, teaching students how to meet fixed deadlines is an important step in preparing youngsters for the demands of higher education or the workplace. Showing students that fixed deadlines are, indeed, part of the real world, and that they can progress at their own pace so long as these target dates are met helps many teenagers set goals and time limits. Such understanding gives students an advantage in future environments where professors or employers rarely spend time discussing these issues.

Beyond students recognizing that academic blogs carry with them cutoff dates and language choices, teachers might have to set certain other rules for classroom blogs. An explanation that student participation is mandatory might be needed in the early stages. There may have to be discussions about the types of language or topics students may present on the class blog, depending on the students and their ages. Also, the teacher needs to set clear standards on when students have to post responses or work on the materials of peers. These areas set guidelines for student behavior that can be monitored and evaluated, which assists instructors with ongoing evaluation.

Challenge 4: Integrating Multiple Intelligences to Ensure Self-Directed Learning

A fourth challenge for teachers is to integrate multiple intelligence theory into blogging. While an earlier chapter extensively addresses the need for teachers to consider students' multiple intelligences through blogging, students may have difficulty shaping their own coursework and learning experiences, especially those who are not used to directing their own education. One way that teachers can help students ease into self-directed learning is to create topic sheets that encourage students to pursue diverse perspectives or topics relevant to the course under the teacher's independent guidance.

Another possibility for educators to address multiple intelligence theory in an asynchronous blog is to have students upload individual projects to the class blog. That way, all students can showcase their work to a larger audience, which helps students see their work as having meaning to a wider group.

The overall concept when integrating blogs with multiple intelligence theory is to build upon the multimedia strengths found in electronic genres. All students have the capacity to participate in the blogosphere because all students have something intelligent to offer. Students can highlight their specialties and downplay their weaknesses through skillful blogging on a topic.

Challenge 5: Balancing Information Overload

The fifth challenge that teachers face with blogging in the classroom is the possibility that the students and the teacher will encounter information overload. Because blogged material can be accessed at any time, and the information can either supplement or be directly related to course content, there is a risk that the class can find itself wallowing in a sea of data.

Teachers have to monitor this situation. Blogging should never displace face-to-face connections between instructors and students. Nor should blogging create discontinuity or a lack of immediacy of course material in the classroom. Blogs should supplement or extend, not replace a teacher-student relationship. As an asynchronous mode for learning, blogs make learning more flexible and responsive to students' interests and needs outside of the classroom. Blogs are a way to reestablish a joy or a desire to learn beyond traditional class experiences.

Blogging challenges teachers and students to see the learning experience as something beyond a forty-five-minute class period or a ninety-minute block of time to fill. For students who cannot always be present in a traditional classroom because of illness, suspension, family or work obligations, blogs offer a way for them to demonstrate that they can learn under an alternative method. Students who are not always on top of their game in a traditional classroom can repair their academic reputations by shining on a blog. A class blog provides bored students a chance to show other students new or cool items related to the class content that would be dismissed under the usual time constraints. That is why a blog is only as good as the blogger or teacher who builds it. The ultimate challenge for a teacher blogger is to create the killer app—the "kewlest" blog—one that generates effective learning for the classroom.

The coolest teacher is not necessarily the one who has the greatest amount of technological know-how but the one who knows how to manipulate the technology to achieve the greatest result with students.

HOW TO MAKE BLOGGING MATTER IN SCHOOLS

Perhaps after reading slightly fewer than two hundred pages about blogging and its effect on students and learning, some parents, teachers, and administrators are ready to design a plan to institute blogging as a part of the curriculum. The question for these individuals becomes, how can they make blogging matter in students' day-to-day learning?

I believe for blogging to truly take hold as a curricular cornerstone, parents, teachers, and administrators will need to work in concert. That is why this last section of the book addresses each of these group separately, as every one of these groups has something significant to contribute to the overall curricular goals.

Since school administrators have the power to carry out curricular actions in the schools they lead, I will start with them. In these times of budget constraints, most administrators cringe at wide-scale changes in curriculum because of the high costs that some of these reforms carry.

But school administrators are also what I like to call Chief Culture Organizers (COOs). As a COO, the administrator is responsible for molding or changing school culture to reflect a vital learning environment. The trick is for the COO to institute progressive changes that incorporate new forms of literacy without inflicting damage on shrinking school budgets.

What I propose here is not a financial burden on schools. It is a rethinking of what can be done in the present curriculum and in terms of leadership. The five areas where school administrators can evince curricular change using blogging without burdening taxpayers are as follows:

1. Ensure that Internet access is available to all students throughout the day, including before and after school periods. Encourage students from disadvantaged backgrounds to spend time on the Internet to work on their blogs. Use free educational blog-hosting sites or have the district educational technology specialist investigate the use of low-cost blog software like Moveable Type or Manilla.

2. Establish that students and teachers have at least one blog-based assignment each marking period. Visit class blogs and leave posts to ensure that students and teachers realize that the administration pays attention to their online learning environment.

3. Provide an on-site system that addresses teachers' deficiencies with blogging, wiki building, podcasting, and other similar technology. Contact area colleges or universities for experts in writing and technology. Most college or university writing programs have faculty who would be happy to conduct professional development workshops on blogging, wiki building, podcasting, and other topics for K–12 or K–13 teachers.

4. Maintain a blog for the school district as part of the district's web presence. The blog can be a dynamic site where photos of school activities, athletics, and announcements as well as examples of fine student work can be showcased. These items can be uploaded quickly and changed as needed.

5. Make sure faculty evaluations include a section on current use of technology, such as blogs, wikis, or podcasts in the classroom. If

school administrators take blogging seriously as a curricular component, they will evaluate the activity. If teachers take blogging seriously and see the administration cares enough about the activity to make it part of a teacher's professional evaluation, they also will incorporate blogging into their day.

Teachers have a place in this discussion as well. Their days are often filled with endless paper shuffling, disciplinary concerns, and classroom management. Still, blogging can become a core activity in a teacher's class without being burdensome to the faculty member. Here are five areas that teachers can focus on to make blogging a part of their day-to-day lesson plans:

1. Work with curriculum supervisors to create technology fairs that showcase student blogs, wikis, or podcasts for the general public.
2. Ask school administrators for professional in-service workshops that not only show teachers how to build blogs, wikis, or podcasts but also address current pedagogical uses of these electronic genres. Or, enroll in graduate classes at local universities where technology is integrated with pedagogy or with content area learning—most medium to large universities offer these courses for graduate students. Incorporate this material into a professional development plan to become highly qualified.
3. Encourage school personnel and parents to visit your class blog, wiki, or podcast to leave messages for students.
4. Work with school librarians to establish media center schedules to accommodate students before and after school as well as during lunch or other free periods throughout the day. This helps students who have limited access to computers outside of school stay on task.
5. Develop rubrics that focus on information literacy, especially those related to multimedia (blog) use. Center the rubric on information seeking and gathering, finding information within sources, evaluating effective sources, extracting pertinent information from selected sources, synthesizing the pertinent information in new and appropriate ways (blogs, wikis, podcasts, and so on), and the effectiveness of the presentation of synthesized materials.

Without parents' support, blogging may not be incorporated into the curriculum. Parents have a powerful voice in their local schools, although it might not always seem that way. For parents who want to help their children become technologically literate in using effective asynchronous learning tools like blogs, here are five areas to focus on:

1. Take an interest in your child's online activities. Visit their blogs, MySpace accounts (all of them, not just the ones the kids tell you they have), and websites. Talk to your youngsters about their online experiences, good or bad.

2. Ask the local parent-teacher organization to sponsor a technology fair or technology night out where the community can see what students are doing with regard to blogs, wikis, podcasts, websites, or new electronic genres.

3. When visiting your child's teacher, ask whether students blog in class. If they aren't blogging, ask why. If you're technologically skilled, offer your services as a teacher technology aide who can assist students (and the teacher) in developing blogs, wikis, or other asynchronous genres for learning.

4. Ask whether students have an online portfolio of their class work that parents can access. If there is no such portfolio, ask the teachers or school administrators why students do not have electronic portfolios. Perhaps the class has an evaluation sheet that specifically addresses blogging, wikis, or other asynchronous learning activities. Ask to see those rubrics. If none exist, ask why these items do not exist. Explain that it is crucial for youngsters to learn how to submit their assignments electronically at some point in their studies to prepare them for college or for work, where sending documents via email or other electronic means is standard procedure.

5. Ask teachers and administrators during conference time what they are doing to keep current with blogs, wikis, podcasts, or other asynchronous learning environments. Ask whether a code of ethics or an honor code for student blogging exists. Show the district that you have a strong interest in 21st-century literacy learning.

It is possible to have the schools we want—schools that prepare young students to enter college or the workforce with the information literacy

tools and skills professors and employers expect. Blogging matters because it is the first electronic genre since e-mail that has changed the
way people write, think, and process information. If we expect students
to graduate from twelve or thirteen years of schooling with the technological competencies needed to enter higher education or industry, then
we have to ensure that K–12 or K–13 schools deliver.

My hope is that blogs and their multimedia complements do not go
the way of the television. My parents' generation never fully understood
the power of the TV. Certainly the *New York Times'* editorial staff failed
to understand the appeal of TV when in 1939 it stated in an editorial
that the average American family has no time for television, that people
must sit and keep their eyes glued on a screen. This principle dominated
life throughout the 1950s and shaped an entire generation. Viewers did
glue their eyes on a screen. The average American family made time for
television.

As a result, today most of us have five hundred channels of dross fill-
ing the airwaves and acting like an electronic babysitter. Teenagers and
young adults realize this and they have turned to the Internet for their
news, entertainment, and socialization. The Internet is active, dynamic,
and maneuverable. Youngsters have connected to what the late British
novelist Douglas Adams (1999) observed about the Internet: "A computer terminal is not some clunky old television with a typewriter in
front of it. It is an interface where the mind and body can connect with
the universe and move bits of it about." Douglas Adams was right: The
Internet, blogs and all, is alive.

Because of its interface and the ability to transmit knowledge, the
genres created from the Internet have allowed users to expand their
understanding about the world around them. Blogging, wikis, podcasts,
and whatever comes next have the same type of power to educate, to
shape youngsters' minds, and expand their worlds. Unlike the boob
tube, these newer electronic genres are active rather than passive
media. These forms demand users who can manipulate data, evaluate
content, and distribute new knowledge. Blogs and other multimedia
tools are not electronic babysitters or teenage games. Quite the contrary, these multimedia genres are how we communicate successfully in
the 21st century. Not to use these tools puts us at a great disadvantage
in the world. As investor and entrepreneur Prince Alwaleed Bin Talal

Alsaud has been quoted as saying, "Nowadays, anyone who cannot speak English and is incapable of using the Internet is regarded as backward" (2005).

That is why blogging matters. For students to succeed in the future, they should be masters of their native tongue and of the genres found on the Internet. That is because our students are the Internet. These days, students need to be proactive in their approaches to learning and to the world in which they live. The best place for students to learn these ideas is in school under the guidance and direction of trained teachers who can talk about the importance of language, the Internet, and the centrality of both to our lives in the 21st century.

When done well, blogs teach us that communicating is far more than having our eyes glued on a screen and that reaching out to the world through our computers is more than having a pseudo-TV connected to a quasi-typewriter. Perhaps this book will open a new dialogue between educators and students—as well as between parents and students—as to why blogging matters for the youngsters in their lives. Blogging could be the start of how highly globalized societies educate their young in an information-driven, technology-infused society. Through blogging, students may be leading the rest of us into a new awareness of what might be possible for delivering literacy instruction via the Internet.

On the other hand, it might be simply that blogging presents tweens and teens with the opportunity to make meaning out of their lives, perhaps not as freely as they might always wish, but certainly not as the victims of their own circumstances. Through such conversations, adults may discover that blogging offers one small but highly public window into adolescents' lives. That too may be a good thing.

Then again, none of us will know for sure until we unglue our eyes from older technologies and start asking students why they blog. Because with increasing regularity each day, it seems as though blogging certainly matters to them.

REFERENCES

Adams, D. (1999, August 29). *How to stop worrying and learn to love the Internet.* Retrieved December 7, 2006, from www.douglasadams.com/dna/19990901-00-a.html.

Aftab, P. (1999). *Cyber911 emergency.* Retrieved March 14, 2006, from www.wiredsafety.org.

Associated Press. (2005, November 6). *Orange county gunman was outcast.* File report. Retrieved July 2006, from www.blogs.kansascity.com/crime_scene/2005/11/what_to_do_with.html.

Beaumont, M. (2006, April 7). Star wars kid: Un règlement hors cour. *Corus Nouvelles Regional.* Retrieved December 7, 2006, from www.corusnouvelles.com/nouvelle-star_wars_kid_-10775-4.html.

Bin Talal Alsaud, A. (2005). Retrieved December 11, 2006, from www.woopidoo.com/business_quotes/authors/prince-alwaleed-quotes.htm.

British Broadcasting Corporation. (1999, November 15). *UK: Girls more assertive than boys.* Retrieved December 7, 2006, from news.bbc.co.uk/2/hi/uk_news/517623.stm.

British Broadcasting Corporation. (2003, November 4). *Boys seek help at breaking point.* Retrieved December 7, 2006, from news.bbc.co.uk/2/hi/uk_news/3238909.stm.

British Broadcasting Corporation. (2005, November 8). *Gender divide in getting the joke.* Retrieved January 2007, from news.bbc.co/uk/1/hi/health/4413790.stm.

Bruner, J. (1960). *The process of education.* New York: Vintage Books.

CBS News. (2005, November 6). *Orange County gunman was outcast.* Retrieved July 2006, from www.cbsnews.com/stories/2005/11/06/ap/national/mainD8DN1S800.shtml.

Citizen Voices. (2006). Blog. Available at www.citizenvoices.gg.ca.

Countdown with Keith Olbermann. (2006). *Most viral video ever.* MSNBC. Available at www.msnbc.msn.com/id/15958470/.

Crick, N. R., Casas, J. F., & Ku, H. C. (1999). Relational and physical forms of victimization in preschool. *Developmental Psychology 35,* 376–85.

Cszikszentmihalyi, M. (1990). *Flow: The psychology of optimal experience.* New York: HarperCollins.

Cszikszentmihalyi, M. (1997). *Creativity: Flow and the psychology of discovery and invention.* New York: Harper Perennial.

Davis, A. (2004). Ways to use weblogs in the classroom. *E-school news tech insider newsletter.* Retrieved October 5, 2004, from www.eschoolnews.com/eti/2004/10/000180.php.

Elbow, P. (1973). *Writing without teachers.* New York: Oxford University Press.

Electronic Frontier Foundation. (2006, April 20). EFF: Legal guide for bloggers. Retrieved January 2007, from eff.org/bloggers/1g.

Ellickson, P. L. (2000). Tranquilizing effect. *RAND Review.* Retrieved December 7, 2006, from www.rand.org/publications/randreview/issues/rr.12.00/tranquil.html.

Fallows, D. (2004). *The Internet and daily life.* Retrieved December 7, 2006, from www.pewinternet.org/PPF/r/131/report_display.asp.

Feuer, A., & George, J. (2005, Februrary 26). Internet fame is cruel mistress for dancer of the Numa Numa. *Globe and Mail.* Retrieved December 7, 2006, from www.globeandmail.com.

Fox, S. (2006). *Blogging with middle school students.* Unpublished manuscript. Rowan University.

Gardner, H. (1993). *Frames of mind: The theory of multiple intelligences.* New York: Basic Books.

Gardner, H. (1999). *Intelligence reframed: Multiple intelligences for the 21st century.* New York: Basic Books.

Graves, D. (2003). *Testing is not teaching: What should count in education.* Portsmouth, NH: Heinemann.

Griswold, W., McDonnell, T., & Wright, N. (2005). Reading and the reading class in the twenty-first century. *Annual Review of Sociology 31,* 127–41.

Ha, T. T. (2003, July 3). Parents file lawsuit over Star Wars video. *Globe and Mail,* p. A2.

Hahn, M. (2005, November 14). A loaded discussion. *The Guardian Unlimited.* Retrieved December 7, 2006, from www.guardian.co.uk/usguns/Story/0,,1642081,00.html.

Henderson, T. (2001, September/October). Classroom assessment techniques in asynchronous learning networks. *The Technology Source*. Retrieved December 7, 2006, from technologysource.org/article/classroom_assessment_technique_in_asynchronouslearning_networks/.

Hepp, P., Hinostroza, E., Laval, E., & Rehbein, L. (2005). *Technology in schools: Education, ICT and the knowledge society*. Retrieved January 2007, from siteresources.worldbank.org/education/resources.

Herring, S. (1996). Posting in a different voice. *Philosophical Perspectives on Computer-Mediated Communication*, ed. Charles Ess. Albany, NY: SUNY Press.

Huffaker, D. (2004). *Gender similarities and differences in online identity and language use among teenage bloggers*. Unpublished master's thesis. Georgetown University: Washington, DC.

Hunter, A. (2005, December 1). *When murder hits the blogosphere*. Retrieved December 7, 2006, from www.msnbc.msn.com/id/10272868/.

Kear, K., & Heap, N. (1999). Technology-supported groupwork in distance learning. *Active Learning* 10. Available at www.ilt.ac.uk/public/cti/Active Learning/al10pdf/Kear.heap [pdf].

Kress, G., & van Leeuwen, T. (2003). *Multimodal discourse*. Oxon, UK: Hodder Arnold.

Lankshear, C., & Knobel, M. (2003). *New Literacies*. London: Open University Press.

Lenhart, A., & Madden, M. (2005). *Teen content creators and consumers*. November 2, 2005. Available at www.pewinternet.org.

Lenhart, A., Madden, M., & Hitlin, P. (2005). *Teens and technology*. Retrieved December 7, 2006, from www.pewinternet.org/report_display.asp?r = 162.

Liu, A. (2005). *The laws of cool: Knowledge work and the culture of information*. Chicago: University of Chicago Press.

Nardi, B. A., Schiano, D. J., Gumbrecht, M., & Swartz, L. (2004). Why we blog. *Communications of the ACM* 47(12), December 2004, 41–46.

National Center for Educational Statistics. (2004). *The Nation's Report Card*. Retrieved January 2007, from nces.ed.gov/nationsreportcard/.

Nelson, D. A., Robinson, C. C., & Hart, C. H. (2005). Relational and physical aggression of preschool-age children: Peer status linkages across informants. *Early education and development* 16(2), 115–40.

Newkirk, T. (2002). *Misreading masculinities*. Portsmouth, NH: Heinemann.

Pappas, L. A. (2005, January 2). High tech harassment hitting teens hard. *Philadelphia Inquirer*, A1.

Penrod, D. (2005). *Composition in convergence*. Mahwah, NJ: Lawrence Erlbaum Associates.

Pollack, W. (2000). *Real boys' voices.* New York: Owl Books.

Prichard, O. (2005, December 11). Danger: Teen web networks. *Philadelphia Inquirer,* p. A1.

Rainie, L. (2004). *The state of blogging.* Retrieved December 7, 2006, from www.pewinternet.org/PPF/r/144/report_display.asp

Selfe, C., & Meyer, P. (1991). Testing claims for on-line conferences. *Written Communication* 8(2), 162–92.

Smith, M. W., & Wilhelm, J. (2002). *Reading don't fix no Chevys.* Portsmouth, NH: Heinemann.

Smith, P. (2005). *Tackling cyberbullying.* Available at www.anti-cyberbullyingalliance.org.uk.

Stroud, R., Graham, K., Zayas, A., & Thompson, J. (2005, December 23). Concerns lead to worst nightmare. *St. Petersburg Times.* Retrieved December 7, 2006, from www.sptimes.com/2005/12/23/Hillsborough/Concerns_lead_to_wors.shtml.

Syverson, M. (2000). *A wealth of reality.* Carbondale: Southern Illinois University Press.

Tannen, D. (1990). *Conversational style: Analyzing talk among friends.* Mahwah, NJ: Ablex.

Thomas, W. P., & Collier, V. (1997). *School effectiveness for language minority students.* Washington, DC: National Clearinghouse for Bilingual Education.

Voss, G. (2006, January). *Boston* magazine. Retrieved December 7, 2006, from www.bostonmagazine.com/articles/meankidscom.

Vygotsky, L. (1978). *Mind in society: The development of higher mental processes.* Cambridge, MA: Harvard University Press.

Walton, A. (1999, January). Technology versus African Americans. *The Atlantic.* Available at www.theatlantic.com.

Wenger, E., McDermott, R., & Snyder, W. M. (2002). *Cultivating communities of practice.* Cambridge, MA: Harvard University Press.

Wired News. (2003, July 24). *Star Wars Kid files lawsuit.* Available at www.wired.com/news/culture/0,59757-0.html?tw=wn_tophead_4.

Wiredsafety.org. (2005). *Internet 101.* Retrieved January 2007, from wiredsafety.org/internet101/blogs.html.

Whitely, J. (2005, October 31). When teasing isn't funny: The cost of bullying. *Las Vegas Review-Journal.* Retrieved December 7, 2006, from www.reviewjournal.com/lvrj_home/2005/Oct-31-Mon-2005/living/4038822.html.

Whithaus, C. (2005). *Teaching and evaluating writing in an age of computers and high stakes testing.* Mahwah, NJ: Lawrence Erlbaum Associates.

SUBJECT INDEX

adolescent identities, 14, 50, 57–59, 92, 117

Africentric theory, 74

alternative assessment, 126–27

American economy, viii

Asian teens and blogging, 63

at-risk students, 25, 28–30, 70, 72–74

audioblogs, 28, 152

autotelic behavior (autotelism), 9–10

authentic voice, 16

bloggerel, definition, 50

blogging safely, 93–119

blog ring, definition, 60

blogs, definition, 1

blogs and "flow," 7

"body-less" communication, 26

bullying and blogs, 77–95

codes of ethics for blogging, 139–49

common experiences, 106–12

cooperative learning, 22–23, 31

critical thinking, 23

cross-curricular learning, 24

cultural lag, 2

cyberbullying, 78–85

cyberbullying and boys, 89–90

deaf students and blogging, 27

digital natives/digital immigrants, 98–99, 114, 130

ESL and ELL students, 25, 30

ethics and blogging in schools, 139–49

ethnicity and blogging, 63–74

feminine style, 50–51, 54–56, 59–60

flaming, definition, 50

friendships and blogging, 58

gatekeepers, 4

gender and blogging, 49–62

griefer, definition, 83

"hipness factor" in blogging, 64–66

IM speak, 114

Information Age, viii

Information and Communication Technologies (ICT), ix, 152

"information illiterate," 19

information literacy, 60, 62, 109, 153, 159–60

knowledge economy, viii

Latino and latina teens, 63

leet speak, definition, 135

linguistic code switching, 134–35

literacy, traditional, 19, 27, 32, 61, 73, 151

masculine style, 49–52, 54–56

memes, 11

minority students and blogging, 66–76

multiple intelligences theory, 119–37, 159

"notify wars" ("warning war"), 83

parents and safe blogging, 112–15

peer mediation, 103–5

peer socialization, 57

relational aggression, 81–90, 118

special needs students, 25

spiral curriculum, 128

storytelling, 16, 21

telephone, 55–56

television, x, 95–96, 130, 164–65

transferable skills, 119

trolling, definition, 50

visually impaired students and blogging, 28

wikis, 60, 152, 164

writing, 20–22, 24, 66, 68–70, 199–21, 132

write to learn, 25

zone of proximal development, 31, 33

NAME INDEX

Adams, Douglas, 164
Aftab, Parry, 78, 80–81, 115
Alsaud, Alwaleed Bin Talal, 164–65
Associated Press, 89
Arceo, Linda, 112, 114
Banneker, Benjamin, 67
Bebo, 15
Bethlehem Steel, vii
Blogger, 5, 15
Borden, Kara, 13, 15
Boston magazine, 85
Brinkmann, Melissa, 131–36
British Broadcasting Corporation, 89
Bruner, Jerome, 128
Buffalo Forge, vii
Cargill, vii
Carver, George Washington, 67
CBS News, 88
Colbert, Stephen, vii, viii, ix
Countdown with Keith Olbermann, 88
Cszikszentmihalyi, Mihalyi, 7, 127–28, 130
Davis, Miles, 67
Dungy, James, 13, 15
Elbow, Peter, 21

Ellickson, P. L., 91
Fox, Stefanie, 131–36
Freund, William, 85, 88–89
Gardner, Howard, 119, 121–23, 132
General Electric, vii
Giovanni, Nikki, 67
Golding, William, 67
Google, 27, 116
Graves, Donald, 132
Guevara, Che, 67
Halligan, Ryan, 85–86
Heap, Karen, 59
Henderson, T., 156
Herring, Susan, 56
Hodge, Margaret, 89
Huffaker, David, 52–54, 56, 59
Hughes, Langston, 67
JotSpot, 11
KaZaA, 87
Kear, K., 59
Knobel, Michele, 65
Knox College, vii
Knowles, John, 67
Kobert, Leigh, 26
Kress, Gunther, 131–32
Kyi, Aung San Suu, 67
Lankshear, Colin, 65

Las Vegas Review Journal, 85
Lenhart, Amanda, 17, 112
Liu, Alan, 65
LiveJournal, 14, 102
Ludwig, David, 14
Medville, Karen, 67
Meyer, Paul, 56
Moveable Type, 5
MySpace, 5, 13–15, 96, 102, 112, 114, 117, 163
National Assessment of Educational Progress (NAEP), 65
Newkirk, Thomas, 90
New York Times, 164
NiceNet.org, 131
Pelletier, Leonard, 67
Penrod, Diane, 156
Philadelphia Inquirer, 85, 96
Polites, Olga, 131–32, 135–36
Pollack, William, 53
Rainie, Lee, 6, 17, 63
Raza, Ghyslain, 85–87, 90

Revels, Hiram Rhodes, 67
Selfe, Cindy, 56
Smith, Michael W., 53
Smith, Peter, 78, 80
SomethingAwful.com, 88
Stark, Zach, 14–15
Syverson, Margaret, 156
Tannen, Deborah, 57
Toronto Globe and Mail, 87
van Leeuwen, Theo, 131
Vygotsky, Lev, 31
Walton, Anthony, 75
WebCrimson, 5
Whithaus, Carl, 156
Wikipedia, 60
Wilhelm, Jeffrey, 53
WiredNews, 87
WiredSafety.org, 16
World Bank, ix
Wounded Knee, 67
Wrongplanet.net, 88
Xanga, 5, 14–15

ABOUT THE AUTHOR

Diane Penrod (B.S. in media and communication from Medaille College, Buffalo, N.Y.; M.Ed. in English education from SUNY Oswego, Oswego, N.Y.; M.A. in linguistics from Syracuse University, Syracuse, N.Y.; and Ph.D. in English composition and cultural rhetoric from Syracuse University) is professor of writing arts at Rowan University in Glassboro, N.J. She directs the master's program in writing and is the site director for the National Writing Project at Rowan. Dr. Penrod was named a 2000 Outstanding Young Scholar in Postmodern Theory by IBC London.